JAMESTOWN EDUCATION

Timed Readings Plus *in Science*

25 Two-Part Lessons
with Questions for
Building Reading Speed and Comprehension

BOOK 9

Glencoe
McGraw-Hill

New York, New York   Columbus, Ohio   Chicago, Illinois   Peoria, Illinois   Woodland Hills, California

JAMESTOWN EDUCATION

Glencoe/McGraw-Hill

A Division of The McGraw·Hill Companies

ISBN: 0-07-827378-1

Send all queries to:
Glencoe/McGraw-Hill
8787 Orion Place
Columbus, OH 43240-4027

1 2 3 4 5 6 7 8 9 10 021 08 07 06 05 04 03 02

CONTENTS

To the Student

You probably talk at an average rate of about 150 words a minute. If you are a reader of average ability, you read at a rate of about 250 words a minute. So your reading speed is nearly twice as fast as your speaking or listening speed. This example shows that reading is one of the fastest ways to get information.

The purpose of this book is to help you increase your reading rate and understand what you read. The 25 lessons in this book will also give you practice in reading science articles and in preparing for tests in which you must read and understand nonfiction passages within a certain time limit.

Reading Faster and Better

Following are some strategies that you can use to read the articles in each lesson.

Previewing

Previewing before you read is a very important step. This helps you to get an idea of what a selection is about and to recall any previous knowledge you have about the subject. Here are the steps to follow when previewing.

Read the title. Titles are designed not only to announce the subject but also to make the reader think. Ask yourself questions such as What can I learn from the title? What thoughts does it bring to mind?

What do I already know about this subject?

Read the first sentence. If they are short, read the first two sentences. The opening sentence is the writer's opportunity to get your attention. Some writers announce what they hope to tell you in the selection. Some writers state their purpose for writing; others just try to get your attention.

Read the last sentence. If it is short, read the final two sentences. The closing sentence is the writer's last chance to get ideas across to you. Some writers repeat the main idea once more. Some writers draw a conclusion—this is what they have been leading up to. Other writers summarize their thoughts; they tie all the facts together.

Skim the entire selection. Glance through the selection quickly to see what other information you can pick up. Look for anything that will help you read fluently and with understanding. Are there names, dates, or numbers? If so, you may have to read more slowly.

Reading for Meaning

Here are some ways to make sure you are making sense of what you read.

Build your concentration. You cannot understand what you read if you are not concentrating. When you discover that your thoughts are straying, correct the situation right away. Avoid distractions and distracting situations. Keep in mind the information you learned from previewing. This will help focus your attention on the selection.

Read in thought groups. Try to see meaningful combinations of words—phrases, clauses, or sentences. If you look at only one word at a time (called word-by-word reading), both your comprehension and your reading speed suffer.

Ask yourself questions. To sustain the pace you have set for yourself and to maintain a high level of concentration and comprehension, ask yourself questions such as What does this mean? or How can I use this information? as you read.

Finding the Main Ideas

The paragraph is the basic unit of meaning. If you can quickly discover and understand the main idea of each paragraph, you will build your comprehension of the selection.

Find the topic sentence. The topic sentence, which contains the main idea, often is the first sentence of a paragraph. It is followed by sentences that support, develop, or explain the main idea. Sometimes a topic sentence comes at the end of a paragraph. When it does, the supporting details come first, building the base for the topic sentence. Some paragraphs do not have a topic sentence; all of the sentences combine to create a meaningful idea.

Understand paragraph structure. Every well-written paragraph has a purpose. The purpose may be to inform, define, explain or illustrate. The purpose should always relate to the main idea and expand on it. As you read each paragraph, see how the body of the paragraph tells you more about the main idea.

Relate ideas as you read. As you read the selection, notice how the writer puts together ideas. As you discover the relationship between the ideas, the main ideas come through quickly and clearly.

Mastering Reading Comprehension

Reading fast is not useful if you don't remember or understand what you read. The two exercises in Part A provide a check on how well you have understood the article.

Recalling Facts

These multiple-choice questions provide a quick check to see how well you recall important information from the article. As you learn to apply the reading strategies described earlier, you should be able to answer these questions more successfully.

Understanding Ideas

These questions require you to think about the main ideas in the article. Some main ideas are stated in the article; others are not. To answer some of the questions, you need to draw conclusions about what you read.

The five exercises in Part B require multiple answers. These exercises provide practice in applying comprehension and critical-thinking skills that you can use in all your reading.

Recognizing Words in Context

Always check to see whether the words around an unfamiliar word—its context—can give you a clue to the word's meaning. A word generally appears in a context related to its meaning.

Suppose, for example, that you are unsure of the meaning of the word *expired* in the following passage:

> Vera wanted to check out a book, but her library card had expired. She had to borrow my card, because she didn't have time to renew hers.

You could begin to figure out the meaning of *expired* by asking yourself a question such as, What could have happened to Vera's library card that would make her need to borrow someone else's card? You might realize that if Vera had to renew her card, its usefulness must have come to an end or run out. This would lead you to conclude that the word *expired* must mean "to come to an end" or "to run out." You would be right. The context suggested the meaning.

Context can also affect the meaning of a word you already know. The word *key*, for instance, has many meanings. There are musical keys, door keys, and keys to solving a mystery. The context in which the word *key* occurs will tell you which meaning is correct.

Sometimes a word is explained by the words that immediately follow it. The subject of a sentence and your knowledge about that subject might also help you determine the meaning of an unknown word. Try to decide the meaning of the word *revive* in the following sentence:

> Sunshine and water will revive those drooping plants.

The compound subject is *sunshine* and *water*. You know that plants need light and water to survive and that drooping plants are not healthy. You can figure out that *revive* means "to bring back to health."

Distinguishing Fact from Opinion

Every day you are called upon to sort out fact and opinion. Because much of what you read and hear contains both facts and opinions, you need to be able to tell the two apart.

Facts are statements that can be proved true. The proof must be objective and verifiable. You must be able to check for yourself to confirm a fact.

Look at the following facts. Notice that they can be checked for accuracy and confirmed. Suggested sources for verification appear in parentheses.

- Abraham Lincoln was the 16th president of the United States. (Consult biographies, social studies books, encyclopedias, and similar sources.)

- Earth revolves around the Sun. (Research in encyclopedias or astronomy books; ask knowledgeable people.)

- Dogs walk on four legs. (See for yourself.)

Opinions are statements that cannot be proved true. There is no objective evidence you can consult to check the truthfulness of an opinion. Unlike facts, opinions express personal beliefs or judgments. Opinions reveal how someone feels about a subject, not the facts about that subject. You might agree or disagree with someone's opinion, but you cannot prove it right or wrong.

Look at the following opinions. The reasons these statements are classified as opinions appear in parentheses.

- Abraham Lincoln was born to be a president. (You cannot prove this by referring to birth records. There is no evidence to support this belief.)

- Earth is the only planet in our solar system where intelligent life exists. (There is no proof of this. It may be proved true some day, but for now it is just an educated guess—not a fact.)

- The dog is a human's best friend. (This is not a fact; your best friend might not be a dog.)

As you read, be aware that facts and opinions are often mixed together. Both are useful to you as a reader. But to evaluate what you read and to read intelligently, you need to know the difference between the two.

Keeping Events in Order

Sequence, or chronological order, is the order of events in a story or article or the order of steps in a process. Paying attention to the sequence of events or steps will help you follow what is happening, predict what might happen next, and make sense of a passage.

To make the sequence as clear as possible, writers often use signal words to help the reader get a more exact idea of when things happen. Following is a list of frequently used signal words and phrases:

until	first
next	then
before	after
finally	later
when	while
during	now
at the end	by the time
as soon as	in the beginning

Signal words and phrases are also useful when a writer chooses to relate details or events out of sequence. You need to pay careful attention to determine the correct chronological order.

Making Correct Inferences

Much of what you read *suggests* more than it *says*. Writers often do not state ideas directly in a text. They can't. Think of the time and space it would take to state every idea. And think of how boring that would be! Instead, writers leave it to you, the reader, to fill in the information they leave out—to make inferences. You do this by combining clues in the story or article with knowledge from your own experience.

You make many inferences every day. Suppose, for example, that you are visiting a friend's house for the first time. You see a bag of kitty litter. You infer (make an inference) that the family has a cat. Another day you overhear a conversation. You catch the names of two actors and the words *scene, dialogue,* and *directing.* You infer that the people are discussing a movie or play.

In these situations and others like them, you infer unstated information from what you observe or read. Readers must make inferences in order to understand text.

Be careful about the inferences you make. One set of facts may suggest several inferences. Some of these inferences could be faulty. A correct inference must be supported by evidence.

Remember that bag of kitty litter that caused you to infer that your friend has a cat? That could be a faulty inference. Perhaps your friend's family uses the kitty litter on their icy sidewalks to create traction. To be sure your inference is correct, you need more evidence.

Understanding Main Ideas

The main idea is the most important idea in a paragraph or passage—the idea that provides purpose and direction. The rest of the selection explains, develops, or supports the main idea. Without a main idea, there would be only a collection of unconnected thoughts.

In the following paragraph, the main idea is printed in italics. As you read, observe how the other sentences develop or explain the main idea.

Typhoon Chris hit with full fury today on the central coast of Japan. Heavy rain from the storm flooded the area. High waves carried many homes into the sea. People now fear that the heavy rains will cause mudslides in the central part of the country. The number of people killed by the storm may climb past the 200 mark by Saturday.

In this paragraph, the main-idea statement appears first. It is followed by sentences that explain, support, or give details. Sometimes the main idea appears at the end of a paragraph. Writers often put the main idea at the end of a paragraph when their purpose is to persuade or convince. Readers may be more open to a new idea if the reasons for it are presented first.

As you read the following paragraph, think about the overall impact of the supporting ideas. Their purpose is to convince the reader that the main idea in the last sentence should be accepted.

Last week there was a head-on collision at Huntington and Canton streets. Just a month ago a pedestrian was struck there. Fortunately, she was only slightly injured. In the past year, there have been more accidents there than at any other corner in the city. In fact, nearly 10 percent of all accidents in the city occur at the corner. This intersection is very dangerous, and a traffic signal should be installed there before a life is lost.

The details in the paragraph progress from least important to most important. They achieve their full effect in the main idea statement at the end.

In many cases, the main idea is not expressed in a single sentence. The reader is called upon to interpret all of the ideas expressed in the paragraph and to decide upon a main idea. Read the following paragraph.

> The American author Jack London was once a pupil at the Cole Grammar School in Oakland, California. Each morning the class sang a song. When the teacher noticed that Jack wouldn't sing, she sent him to the principal. He returned to class with a note. The note said that Jack could be excused from singing with the class if he would write an essay every morning.

In this paragraph, the reader has to interpret the individual ideas and to decide on a main idea. This main idea seems reasonable: Jack London's career as a writer began with a punishment in grammar school.

Understanding the concept of the main idea and knowing how to find it is important. Transferring that understanding to your reading and study is also important.

Working Through a Lesson

Part A

1. **Preview the article.** Locate the timed selection in Part A of the lesson that you are going to read. Wait for your teacher's signal to preview. You will have 20 seconds for previewing. Follow the previewing steps described on page 2.

2. **Read the article.** When your teacher gives you the signal, begin reading. Read carefully so that you will be able to answer questions about what you have read. When you finish reading, look at the board and note your reading time. Write this time at the bottom of the page on the line labeled Reading Time.

3. **Complete the exercises.** Answer the 10 questions that follow the article. There are 5 fact questions and 5 idea questions. Choose the best answer to each question and put an X in that box.

4. **Correct your work.** Use the Answer Key at the back of the book to check your answers. Circle any wrong answer and put an X in the box you should have marked. Record the number of correct answers on the appropriate line at the end of the lesson.

Part B

1. **Preview and read the passage.** Use the same techniques you

used to read Part A. Think about what you are reading.

2. **Complete the exercises.** Instructions are given for answering each category of question. There are 15 responses for you to record.

3. **Correct your work.** Use the Answer Key at the back of the book. Circle any wrong answer and write the correct letter or number next to it. Record the number of correct answers on the appropriate line at the end of the lesson.

Plotting Your Progress

1. **Find your reading rate.** Turn to the Reading Rate graph on page 116. Put an X at the point where the vertical line that represents the lesson intersects your reading time, shown along the left-hand side. The right-hand side of the graph will reveal your words-per-minute reading speed.

2. **Find your comprehension score.** Add your scores for Part A and Part B to determine your total number of correct answers. Turn to the Comprehension Score graph on page 117. Put an X at the point where the vertical line that represents your lesson intersects your total correct answers, shown along the left-hand side. The right-hand side of the graph will show the percentage of questions you answered correctly.

3. **Complete the Comprehension Skills Profile.** Turn to page 118. Record your incorrect answers for the Part B exercises. The five Part B skills are listed along the bottom. There are five columns of boxes, one column for each question. For every incorrect answer, put an X in a box for that skill.

To get the most benefit from these lessons, you need to take charge of your own progress in improving your reading speed and comprehension. Studying these graphs will help you to see whether your reading rate is increasing and to determine what skills you need to work on. Your teacher will also review the graphs to check your progress.

About the Series

Timed Readings Plus in Science includes 10 books at reading levels 4–13, with one book at each level. Book One contains material at a fourth-grade reading level; Book Two at a fifth-grade level, and so on. The readability level is determined by the Fry Readability Scale and is not to be confused with grade or age level. The books are designed for use with students at middle-school level and above.

The purposes of the series are as follows:

- to provide systematic, structured reading practice that helps students improve their reading rate and comprehension skills

- to give students practice in reading and understanding informational articles in the content area of science

- to give students experience in reading various text types—informational, expository, narrative, and prescriptive

- to prepare students for taking standardized tests that include timed reading passages in various content areas

- to provide materials with a wide range of reading levels so that students can continue to practice and improve their reading rate and comprehension skills

Because the books are designed for use with students at designated reading levels rather than in a particular grade, the science topics in this series are not correlated to any grade-level curriculum. Most standardized tests require students to read and comprehend science passages. This series provides an opportunity for students to become familiar with the particular requirements of reading science. For example, the vocabulary in a science article is important. Students need to know certain words in order to understand the concepts and the information.

Each book in the series contains 25 two-part lessons. Part A focuses on improving reading rate. This section of the lesson consists of a 400-word timed informational article on a science topic followed by two multiple-choice exercises. Recalling Facts includes five fact questions; Understanding Ideas includes five critical-thinking questions.

Part B concentrates on building mastery in critical areas of comprehension. This section consists of a nontimed passage—the "plus" passage—followed by five exercises that address five major comprehension skills. The passage varies in length; its subject matter relates to the content of the timed selection.

Timed Reading and Comprehension

Timed reading is the best-known method of improving reading speed. There is no point in someone's reading at an accelerated speed if the person does not understand what she or he is reading. Nothing is more important than comprehension in reading. The main purpose of reading is to gain knowledge and insight, to understand the information that the writer and the text are communicating.

Few students will be able to read a passage once and answer all of the questions correctly. A score of 70 or 80 percent correct is normal. If the student gets 90 or 100 percent correct, he or she is either reading too slowly or the material is at too low a reading level. A comprehension or critical thinking score of less than 70 percent indicates a need for improvement.

One method of improving comprehension and critical-thinking skills is for the student to go back and study each incorrect answer. First, the student should reread the question carefully. It is surprising how many students get the wrong answer simply because they have not read the question carefully. Then the student should look back in the passage to find the place where the question is answered, reread that part of the passage, and think about how to arrive at the correct answer. It is important to be able to recognize a correct answer when it is embedded in the text. Teacher guidance or class discussion will help the student find an answer.

Speed Versus Comprehension

It is not unusual for comprehension scores to decline as reading rate increases during the early weeks of timed readings. If this happens, students should attempt to level off their speed—but not lower it—and concentrate more on comprehension. Usually, if students maintain the higher speed and concentrate on comprehension, scores will gradually improve and within a week or two be back up to normal levels of 70 to 80 percent.

It is important to achieve a proper balance between speed and comprehension. An inefficient reader typically reads everything at one speed, usually slowly. Some poor readers, however, read rapidly but without satisfactory comprehension. It is important to achieve a balance between speed and comprehension. The practice that this series provides enables students to increase their reading speed while maintaining normal levels of comprehension.

Getting Started

As a rule, the passages in a book designed to improve reading speed should be relatively easy. The student should not have much difficulty with the vocabulary or the subject matter. Don't worry about the passages being too easy; students should see how quickly and efficiently they can read a passage.

Begin by assigning students to a level. A student should start with a book that is one level below his or her current reading level. If a student's reading level is not known, a suitable starting point would be one or two levels below the student's present grade in school.

Introduce students to the contents and format of the book they are using. Examine the book to see how it is organized. Talk about the parts of each lesson. Discuss the purpose of timed reading and the use of the progress graphs at the back of the book.

Timing the Reading

One suggestion for timing the reading is to have all students begin reading the selection at the same time. After one minute, write on the board the time that has elapsed and begin updating it at 10-second intervals (1:00, 1:10, 1:20, etc.). Another option is to have individual students time themselves with a stopwatch.

Teaching a Lesson

Part A

1. Give students the signal to begin previewing the lesson. Allow 20 seconds, then discuss special science terms or vocabulary that students found.

2. Use one of the methods described above to time students as they read the passage. (Include the 20-second preview time as part of the first minute.) Tell students to write down the last time shown on the board or the stopwatch when they finish reading. Have them record the time in the designated space after the passage.

3. Next, have students complete the exercises in Part A. Work with them to check their answers, using the Answer Key that begins on page 114. Have them circle incorrect answers, mark the correct answers, and then record the numbers of correct answers for Part A on the appropriate line at the end of the lesson. Correct responses to eight or more questions indicate satisfactory comprehension and recall.

Part B

1. Have students read the Part B passage and complete the exercises that follow it. Directions are provided with each exercise. Correct responses require deliberation and discrimination.

2. Work with students to check their answers. Then discuss the answers with them and have them record the number of correct answers for Part B at the end of the lesson.

Have students study the correct answers to the questions they answered incorrectly. It is important that they understand why a particular answer is correct or incorrect.

Have them reread relevant parts of a passage to clarify an answer. An effective cooperative activity is to have students work in pairs to discuss their answers, explain why they chose the answers they did, and try to resolve differences.

Monitoring Progress

Have students find their total correct answers for the lesson and record their reading time and scores on the graphs on pages 116 and 117. Then have them complete the Comprehension Skills Profile on page 118. For each incorrect response to a question in Part B, students should mark an X in the box above each question type.

The legend on the Reading Rate graph automatically converts reading times to words-per-minute rates. The Comprehension Score graph automatically converts the raw scores to percentages.

These graphs provide a visual record of a student's progress. This record gives the student and you an opportunity to evaluate the student's progress and to determine the types of exercises and skills he or she needs to concentrate on.

Diagnosis and Evaluation

The following are typical reading rates.

Slow Reader—150 Words Per Minute

Average Reader—250 Words Per Minute

Fast Reader—350 Words Per Minute

A student who consistently reads at an average or above-average rate (with satisfactory comprehension) is ready to advance to the next book in the series.

A column of Xs in the Comprehension Skills Profile indicates a specific comprehension weakness. Using the profile, you can assess trends in student performance and suggest remedial work if necessary.

Changing Views of the Planets

For thousands of years, people have wondered about the objects in the night sky. The earliest civilizations observed that among the stars, which stay in place relative to one another, are certain brightly shining objects that seem to move through the sky. In ancient Greece, wise men tried to explain the movement of these objects, which we call planets. The English word *planet* comes from a Greek word meaning "wanderer."

The Greeks decided the solar system was geocentric: Earth was at the center of the solar system, and the other planets and the Sun revolved around Earth. This theory was accepted for hundreds of years. It was not until the work of Nicolaus Copernicus, Johannes Kepler, and Galileo Galilei in the 16th and 17th centuries that a heliocentric model of the solar system emerged. Copernicus put the Sun at the center of the solar system, Kepler showed that planets move in elliptical orbits, and Galileo used a new invention called the telescope to provide strong support for Copernicus's model.

Our solar system is composed chiefly of the Sun, the planets, the moons that orbit the planets, and asteroids. Although each planet is unique, there are important shared characteristics that separate the planets into groups. On the basis of these similarities, astronomers have classified planets as terrestrial or Jovian.

Terrestrial planets include the four planets closest to the Sun: Mercury, Venus, Earth, and Mars. *Terra* is the Latin word for "earth" or "land." The terrestrial planets are relatively small planets and are composed of rocky material containing heavy elements such as iron and nickel. They have few or no moons. All of these planets show characteristic physical features—such as mountains and valleys—similar to features found on Earth.

The next four planets in relation to the Sun—Jupiter, Saturn, Uranus, and Neptune—are known as the Jovian planets. The word *Jovian* comes from the Latin word for the Roman god Jupiter. These planets are often referred to as the gas giants. They are large and are made up primarily of hydrogen and helium. They are surrounded by rings and have many moons.

Pluto, the planet usually farthest from the Sun, does not fit into either group. Pluto is different from all the other planets and is more like a moon. Because of this, many astronomers do not consider Pluto to be a major planet. Some think it was once a moon of Neptune.

Reading Time _____

Recalling Facts

1. The first person to show that the Sun was at the center of the solar system was
   - ❏ a. Copernicus.
   - ❏ b. Kepler.
   - ❏ c. Galileo.

2. Earth and the planets that resemble it are classified as
   - ❏ a. Jovian.
   - ❏ b. major.
   - ❏ c. terrestrial.

3. Which of the following is a Jovian planet?
   - ❏ a. Mars
   - ❏ b. Jupiter
   - ❏ c. Venus

4. The planet most like a moon is
   - ❏ a. Pluto.
   - ❏ b. Mars.
   - ❏ c. Neptune.

5. According to the article, the Jovian planets are composed primarily of
   - ❏ a. iron and nickel metals.
   - ❏ b. nitrogen and oxygen gases.
   - ❏ c. hydrogen and helium gases.

Understanding Ideas

6. The article implies that the development of scientific knowledge is often limited by
   - ❏ a. the intellectual ability of scientists.
   - ❏ b. available technology.
   - ❏ c. natural curiosity.

7. One can infer from the article that Saturn has more moons than
   - ❏ a. Jupiter.
   - ❏ b. Venus.
   - ❏ c. Uranus.

8. One can infer that *heliocentric* means
   - ❏ a. Earth-centered.
   - ❏ b. Sun-centered.
   - ❏ c. elliptically centered.

9. The fact that the movement of Earth through space is too slow for people to feel probably contributed to the long life of the _____ theory.
   - ❏ a. geocentric
   - ❏ b. heliocentric
   - ❏ c. Keplerian

10. Which of the following would help to explain why Pluto is not considered to be a Jovian planet?
    - ❏ a. It does not have a gaseous composition.
    - ❏ b. It has a larger orbit than Saturn.
    - ❏ c. Sometimes it is closer to the Sun than Neptune is.

The Rings of Saturn

The rings of Saturn are among the most brilliant features of our solar system. They can be seen from Earth with a telescope. Although they appear to be an array of silvery gravel floating freely around Saturn, they are actually composed of pieces of ice ranging in size from small crystals to iceberg-sized chunks.

Despite their seemingly gentle beauty, Saturn's rings contain material that orbits at speeds exceeding 10,000 kilometers per hour (6,200 miles per hour). The closer the rings are to Saturn, the faster they travel.

The ring structures themselves are gigantic; the distance from the inner ring to the outer ring is greater than the distance from Earth to the Moon. There are three main structures, two of which are separated by a distance equivalent to the distance across the United States. But the rings are also amazingly thin: they are no more than a kilometer thick. When two *Voyager* spacecrafts flew by Saturn in the early 1980s, they revealed that each main ring structure actually consists of hundreds of smaller rings called ringlets.

Astronomers have often speculated about how Saturn's rings came into existence. One theory is that two of Saturn's moons collided, leaving a large amount of debris in orbit. Other astronomers think Saturn's rings originated at the same time as the planet but that they were unable to form into moons due to their close proximity to Saturn.

1. **Recognizing Words in Context**

   Find the word *speculated* in the passage. One definition below is closest to the meaning of that word. One definition has the opposite or nearly opposite meaning. The remaining definition has a completely different meaning. Label the definitions C for *closest*, O for *opposite or nearly opposite*, and D for *different*.

   _____ a. guessed

   _____ b. watched

   _____ c. proved

2. **Distinguishing Fact from Opinion**

   Two of the statements below present *facts*, which can be proved correct. The other statement is an *opinion*, which expresses someone's thoughts or beliefs. Label the statements F for *fact* and O for *opinion*.

   _____ a. Saturn has three main ring structures.

   _____ b. Saturn's rings are fascinating to look at through a telescope.

   _____ c. The rings of Saturn are composed of ice.

3. Keeping Events in Order

Label the statements below 1, 2, and 3 to show the order in which the events happened.

_____ a. People first saw Saturn's rings through a telescope.

_____ b. It was discovered that each of Saturn's rings was composed of hundreds of ringlets.

_____ c. The U. S. *Voyager* spacecrafts flew by Saturn in the early 1980s.

4. Making Correct Inferences

Two of the statements below are correct *inferences,* or reasonable guesses. They are based on information in the passage. The other statement is an incorrect, or faulty, inference. Label the statements C for *correct* inference and F for *faulty* inference.

_____ a. Many amateur astronomers have viewed the rings of Saturn.

_____ b. Scientists will one day know for certain how Saturn's rings originated.

_____ c. Before the *Voyager* space flights, no one knew Saturn's rings were composed of hundreds of ringlets.

5. Understanding Main Ideas

One of the statements below expresses the main idea of the passage. One statement is too general, or too broad. The other explains only part of the passage; it is too narrow. Label the statements M for *main idea,* B for *too broad,* and N for *too narrow.*

_____ a. All of the Jovian planets have rings.

_____ b. Saturn's rings have a number of striking characteristics.

_____ c. Saturn's rings are amazingly thin considering their width.

Correct Answers, Part A _____

Correct Answers, Part B _____

Total Correct Answers _____

Earth's crust is made up of material that has existed since the creation of the planet. The crust, which begins at Earth's surface and extends between 5 and 95 kilometers (3 and 60 miles) below, consists of rocks and their components, minerals.

Geologists have identified more than 3,000 different minerals. These range from common substances, such as aluminum, to rare gems, such as diamonds. Despite their differences, all minerals are naturally occurring solids with a regularly repeated pattern of atoms or molecules. This pattern is called the mineral's crystal structure. Crystals can be thought of as structural units, such as cubes, stacked on top of and alongside one another.

Minerals are homogeneous; that is, a mineral consists of only one type of atom or molecule. Minerals that consist entirely of one type of atom are elements. Carbon and sulfur are examples of minerals that are elements. Most minerals are compounds. Compounds consist of one type of molecule. For example, table salt is a mineral compound. Each of its molecules contains one sodium atom and one chlorine atom.

Rocks are formed from various combinations of minerals. Only about 100 different types of minerals—called the rock-forming minerals—are the components of nearly all of the numerous rocks that make up Earth's crust. Rocks are classified into three very broad categories—igneous, sedimentary, and metamorphic. As the material that comprises Earth is recycled over and over, rocks change form.

Igneous rocks crystallize from magma, a mixture of molten minerals and gases that comes from deep within Earth. Crystals form as magma rises to the surface and cools. The more slowly the material rises and cools, the larger the crystals. Quartz, which can be found near the surface, is an example of an igneous rock with large crystals.

Over many years, rocks are subjected to physical and chemical processes that break them apart. These processes are known as weathering and erosion. Weathering and erosion create smaller rock particles that combine with other sediments such as clay and shell particles. Rivers are one of the main creators of deposits of sediment. Sediment deposits solidify over time and form sedimentary rock, the most common type of rock.

Some rock that becomes buried is subjected to high temperatures and pressures. These physical events can create a new, harder type of rock called metamorphic rock. Some of the hardest rocks in nature, such as marble, are metamorphic.

Reading Time _____

Recalling Facts

1. A mineral consists of only
   - ❏ a. one type of atom or molecule.
   - ❏ b. special combinations of pieces of eroded rock.
   - ❏ c. organic compounds.

2. The three main categories of rock are
   - ❏ a. igneous, quartz, and metamorphic.
   - ❏ b. sedimentary, igneous, and metamorphic.
   - ❏ c. sedimentary, mineral, and igneous.

3. An example of a mineral is
   - ❏ a. marble.
   - ❏ b. sedimentary rock.
   - ❏ c. salt.

4. Regularly repeated patterns of atoms or molecules form
   - ❏ a. soil.
   - ❏ b. crystals.
   - ❏ c. sedimentary rock.

5. Geologists have identified more than _____ minerals.
   - ❏ a. 30,000
   - ❏ b. 3,000
   - ❏ c. 45,000

Understanding Ideas

6. Rocks are formed from minerals, which implies that all rocks are
   - ❏ a. elements.
   - ❏ b. naturally occurring.
   - ❏ c. sedimentary.

7. If a builder wanted to use columns made out of rock to hold up the roof of a building, the builder would most likely use
   - ❏ a. igneous rock.
   - ❏ b. sedimentary rock.
   - ❏ c. metamorphic rock.

8. Particles from clamshells are most likely to be incorporated into the structure of
   - ❏ a. igneous rocks.
   - ❏ b. sedimentary rocks.
   - ❏ c. metamorphic rocks.

9. If a person were standing alongside a river and looking at layers of rock in the wall of a canyon, the person would be looking at
   - ❏ a. igneous rock.
   - ❏ b. sedimentary rock.
   - ❏ c. metamorphic rock.

10. From the information in the article, one can infer that rocks containing large crystals are most likely
    - ❏ a. igneous rocks.
    - ❏ b. sedimentary rocks.
    - ❏ c. metamorphic rocks.

2   B   Rock Collecting

People are naturally curious about the world they live in. Some have made hobbies of learning about and identifying aspects of nature they encounter every day. There are birdwatchers and there are butterfly collectors. One of the most popular hobbies involving nature is rock collecting.

Some rock collectors search for valuable gemstones, while others try to find exemplary samples of major types of rock. Still others may be interested in the rocks that are most common in their particular region. Regardless of what a rock collector's goal is, a knowledge of the characteristics of different kinds of rock can help him or her organize a collection. Characteristics that help in rock identification include color, structure, and shininess.

Many good books about rock identification are available. Some have excellent illustrations that show characteristics of different categories of rocks. There are also helpful Web sites that deal with rock collecting. The U.S. Geological Survey, an agency of the federal government, publishes maps that show the geologic characteristics of particular areas. Some cities have clubs or other organizations that promote rock collecting. Whether a person is interested in finding buried treasure in the form of a gemstone or learning more about earth science, rock collecting can be a rewarding hobby.

1. **Recognizing Words in Context**

   Find the word *exemplary* in the passage. One definition below is closest to the meaning of that word. One definition has the opposite or nearly opposite meaning. The remaining definition has a completely different meaning. Label the definitions C for *closest,* O for *opposite or nearly opposite,* and D for *different.*

   _____ a. representative

   _____ b. contrasting

   _____ c. developed

2. **Distinguishing Fact from Opinion**

   Two of the statements below present *facts,* which can be proved correct. The other statement is an *opinion,* which expresses someone's thoughts or beliefs. Label the statements F for *fact* and O for *opinion.*

   _____ a. Rock collecting is a worthwhile activity.

   _____ b. Books have been written about rock identification.

   _____ c. Some rock collectors focus on the rocks of a particular area.

3. Keeping Events in Order

Label the statements below 1, 2, and 3 to show the order in which the events happen.

_____ a. A person borrows a book on rock identification from the library.

_____ b. A person sorts rocks into categories.

_____ c. A person finds some interesting rocks alongside a road.

4. Making Correct Inferences

Two of the statements below are correct *inferences,* or reasonable guesses. They are based on information in the passage. The other statement is an incorrect, or faulty, inference. Label the statements C for *correct* inference and F for *faulty* inference.

_____ a. Some people collect rocks because they enjoy outdoor activities.

_____ b. Students interested in a career in geology can benefit from collecting rocks.

_____ c. Most rock collections feature gemstones.

5. Understanding Main Ideas

One of the statements below expresses the main idea of the passage. One statement is too general, or too broad. The other explains only part of the passage; it is too narrow. Label the statements M for *main idea,* B for *too broad,* and N for *too narrow.*

_____ a. People collect rocks for a variety of reasons.

_____ b. Some people have hobbies that involve nature.

_____ c. There are Web sites that provide information about identifying rocks.

Correct Answers, Part A _____

Correct Answers, Part B _____

Total Correct Answers _____

Within nature, there are definable communities within which groups of organisms interact with one another and with the climate and physical surroundings. These communities are referred to as ecosystems. There are many types of ecosystems: some are aquatic, or water-based, and some are terrestrial, or land-based. A well-known type of terrestrial ecosystem is a rain forest.

One example of an aquatic ecosystem is a pond. Ponds are bodies of water that do not flow or lead to other bodies of water. Because ponds are isolated, the organisms that inhabit them interact with one another as a closed system, meaning they rely on only one another for survival, recycling nutrients from organism to organism.

Nutrient flow within a pond ecosystem is relatively simple. One feature of ponds is that they are shallow enough that water circulates freely at all depths. As a result, photosynthetic algae are abundant in ponds. These algae use the sun's energy to create food, and they produce oxygen as a by-product. They release the oxygen into the pond water, where it is used by other species. Another way that algae benefit a pond ecosystem is by serving as food for other organisms.

Other members of a pond ecosystem include rooted plants, insects, and higher-level species such as frogs, turtles, fish, and birds. Like algae, rooted plants serve as food for animals. Together, algae and rooted plants form the basis of the pond's food web. Energy from the plants is passed through the ecosystem when the plants are eaten by other species and when these species in turn are eaten by birds and fish.

Also important to the pond ecosystem are the microorganisms called decomposers. Decomposers, which in a pond consist mainly of bacteria, eat the remains of dead and decaying organisms. Decomposers live mainly at the bottom of a pond. They play a vital role in the ecosystem; were it not for them, dead organisms would accumulate, causing the pond to become so polluted that all its other organisms would die.

Although ponds are relatively closed ecosystems, some higher-level species can affect the pond from outside the ecosystem. For example, beavers may build a dam on a stream that feeds the pond. This would cut off a source of water that replenishes some of the pond water lost through evaporation. The result would be a shrinking of the pond and a decline in the population of some organisms.

Reading Time _____

Recalling Facts

1. Water-based ecosystems are also known as _____ ecosystems.
   - ❏ a. terrestrial
   - ❏ b. hydro
   - ❏ c. aquatic

2. One way that a pond differs from most other bodies of water is that a pond is more
   - ❏ a. ecological.
   - ❏ b. isolated.
   - ❏ c. active.

3. Life forms that eat dead organisms are called
   - ❏ a. decomposers.
   - ❏ b. herbivores.
   - ❏ c. algae.

4. Pond ecosystems can be described as
   - ❏ a. open.
   - ❏ b. closed.
   - ❏ c. whole.

5. _____ form the foundation of a pond's food web.
   - ❏ a. Plants
   - ❏ b. Fish
   - ❏ c. Birds

Understanding Ideas

6. One can conclude from the article that many pond species rely on _____ for their survival.
   - ❏ a. currents of water
   - ❏ b. the sun
   - ❏ c. higher-level species

7. It can be inferred that if all of the algae in a pond died,
   - ❏ a. organisms that ate algae would begin eating fish instead.
   - ❏ b. many of the other organisms would also die.
   - ❏ c. bacteria would take over the pond.

8. One can infer that the size of a pond varies depending primarily on
   - ❏ a. the amount of rainfall.
   - ❏ b. the number of turtles in the pond.
   - ❏ c. the composition of the mud at the bottom of the pond.

9. The fundamental members of the pond ecosystem are
   - ❏ a. plant-eating organisms.
   - ❏ b. birds and fish.
   - ❏ c. algae and bacteria.

10. A by-product of photosynthesis is
    - ❏ a. fish.
    - ❏ b. oxygen.
    - ❏ c. minerals.

3   B   An Ecosystem in a Barrel

An ecosystem, a self-contained community of organisms together with their environment, can be either land based or water based. For example, a desert is a land-based ecosystem consisting of a dry region inhabited by organisms such as cacti, birds, snakes, and coyotes.

A pond is an example of a water-based ecosystem. Ponds are freestanding bodies of water and may exist in nature wherever there is water that does not evaporate. A pond can be created in a backyard without too much time, expense, or effort.

A simple way to create a pond is with a barrel. To do this, the only necessary ingredients are a leakproof barrel, water, algae, and fish. First, a barrel must be obtained. If the barrel is not leakproof already, it can be made so by covering the inside of it with a sheet of plastic liner. Once the barrel is made leakproof, water can be added. The water used must be free of chemicals that might destroy algae, or the barrel ecosystem will be compromised.

After the water is in the barrel, algae can be introduced. The most convenient source of algae is a pet store, which provides algae for fish tanks. When the algae growth is underway, freshwater fish can be placed into the barrel. If the barrel is stored outside, the standing water may attract mosquitoes that would then also become members of the pond-in-a-barrel ecosystem.

1. Recognizing Words in Context

Find the word *compromised* in the passage. One definition below is closest to the meaning of that word. One definition has the opposite or nearly opposite meaning. The remaining definition has a completely different meaning. Label the definitions C for *closest,* O for *opposite or nearly opposite,* and D for *different.*

_____ a. strengthened

_____ b. refreshed

_____ c. weakened

2. Distinguishing Fact from Opinion

Two of the statements below present *facts,* which can be proved correct. The other statement is an *opinion,* which expresses someone's thoughts or beliefs. Label the statements F for *fact* and O for *opinion.*

_____ a. Creating a pond ecosystem in a barrel is a simple process.

_____ b. A pond is a type of water-based ecosystem.

_____ c. The presence of certain chemicals in water can destroy algae.

3. Keeping Events in Order

Label the statements below 1, 2, and 3 to show the order in which the steps should be completed.

_____ a. Algae are introduced into a pond-in-a-barrel ecosystem.

_____ b. Fish are introduced into a pond-in-a-barrel ecosystem.

_____ c. Water is introduced into a pond-in-a-barrel ecosystem.

4. Making Correct Inferences

Two of the statements below are correct *inferences*, or reasonable guesses. They are based on information in the passage. The other statement is an incorrect, or faulty, inference. Label the statements C for *correct* inference and F for *faulty* inference.

_____ a. Algae provide a food source for fish in the ecosystem.

_____ b. Creating a successful pond-in-a-barrel ecosystem will require hours of study.

_____ c. Mosquitoes are attracted to standing water.

5. Understanding Main Ideas

One of the statements below expresses the main idea of the passage. One statement is too general, or too broad. The other explains only part of the passage; it is too narrow. Label the statements M for *main idea*, B for *too broad*, and N for *too narrow*.

_____ a. A barrel can be used to simulate a natural pond ecosystem.

_____ b. Ecosystems can be either land based or water based.

_____ c. The water used in a pond-in-a-barrel ecosystem must be free of chemicals that can destroy algae.

Correct Answers, Part A _____

Correct Answers, Part B _____

Total Correct Answers _____

The Importance of Photosynthesis

The sun can be considered the ultimate energy source for living things on Earth. Almost all species are dependent—either directly or indirectly—on energy from the sun for their survival. Through a process known as photosynthesis, green plants use the sun's energy to produce food and oxygen. Green plants serve as food for many animals. Even those animals that do not eat plants generally eat animals that do eat plants. Plants thus form the base of Earth's complex food webs.

Photosynthesis is a chemical reaction in which plants take in carbon dioxide and sunlight and combine them with water to produce carbohydrates and oxygen. In most plants, photosynthesis takes place in the leaves.

When the sun's radiant energy reaches a leaf cell, it is absorbed by cellular structures called chloroplasts. Chloroplasts contain chlorophyll, a pigment that reflects green light but absorbs other types of light. As a chlorophyll molecule absorbs sunlight, the energy levels of the molecule's electrons are raised. This extra energy is converted into an energy-carrying compound called ATP. During the creation of ATP, water molecules are split, which releases oxygen into the air.

In the next stage of photosynthesis, ATP combines with carbon dioxide and other substances to form carbohydrates. Because this process involves the transfer of carbon from carbon dioxide to other compounds, it is called carbon fixation. This process is especially significant because it involves the conversion of inorganic compounds to organic compounds. All living things are made of organic compounds.

The final phase of photosynthesis is carbon reduction. This results in the production of such carbohydrates as glucose. Carbohydrates serve as food for plants. They also serve as building blocks for other substances necessary for life. These include amino acids, the components of proteins.

The rate of photosynthesis is affected by such factors as intensity of sunlight, amount of water available to the plant, and temperature. Another factor is the plant itself—some species have a faster rate of photosynthesis than others do. Green plants are not the only organisms that are capable of photosynthesis. Some types of bacteria and protistans are photosynthetic, although the process in these organisms is somewhat different than in green plants.

Without photosynthesis, oxygen would slowly disappear from the atmosphere, and living things would die out from lack of food. It is hard to think of a process more important to life on Earth than photosynthesis.

Reading Time _____

Recalling Facts

1. The process whereby plants convert the sun's energy into carbohydrates is known as
   - ❏ a. autosynthesis.
   - ❏ b. photosynthesis.
   - ❏ c. phototropism.

2. Sunlight is absorbed by a pigment called
   - ❏ a. chloroplast.
   - ❏ b. carbohydrate.
   - ❏ c. chlorophyll.

3. All the following are required for photosynthesis except
   - ❏ a. sunlight.
   - ❏ b. nitrogen-rich fertilizer.
   - ❏ c. water.

4. In addition to oxygen, another product of photosynthesis consists of
   - ❏ a. carbohydrates.
   - ❏ b. carbon dioxide.
   - ❏ c. water.

5. The energy-carrying compound involved in photosynthesis is
   - ❏ a. DNA.
   - ❏ b. ADP.
   - ❏ c. ATP.

Understanding Ideas

6. Since plants take in carbon dioxide and emit oxygen, one could say that their process of gas exchange is _____ that of humans.
   - ❏ a. the reverse of
   - ❏ b. the same as
   - ❏ c. only remotely similar to

7. The process of photosynthesis could be described as the conversion of light energy into _____ energy.
   - ❏ a. mechanical
   - ❏ b. chemical
   - ❏ c. heat

8. One can assume that plants obtain the water required for photosynthesis from
   - ❏ a. air.
   - ❏ b. steam.
   - ❏ c. soil.

9. From the article, one can infer that photosynthetic activity is highest in the
   - ❏ a. summer.
   - ❏ b. fall.
   - ❏ c. spring.

10. One can conclude that a plant that is yellow is likely to have few, if any,
    - ❏ a. carbohydrates.
    - ❏ b. cells.
    - ❏ c. chloroplasts.

Starch is a type of carbohydrate found in various plants. Plants produce starch through the process of photosynthesis, which allows them to store energy until they require it for cellular activities and growth. At that point, plants convert the stored starch into glucose, which can be metabolized for the plant's various requirements.

Starch is white, odorless, and tasteless. To determine whether starch is present in a leaf, perform the following experiment. You will need a potassium iodide solution, one 500mL beaker, one 250mL beaker, a petri dish, a hot plate, a medicine dropper, plastic tongs, isopropyl alcohol, water, and a plant. Since alcohol is flammable, this experiment requires special caution.

Step One: Break a leaf off the plant (with the permission of the plant's owner!).

Step Two: Fill the 500mL beaker with water and the 250mL beaker with alcohol.

Step Three: Put the beaker of alcohol into the beaker of water and place both on the hot plate with the temperature turned to medium high.

Step Four: Drop the plant leaf into the alcohol and heat it for 10 minutes.

Step Five: Using the plastic tongs, remove the leaf and set it in the petri dish.

Step Six: Fill the medicine dropper with potassium iodide and place a few drops of potassium iodide on the leaf.

If the leaf turns purple, then the leaf contains starch. The darker the color of the leaf, the greater the amount of starch it contains.

1. **Recognizing Words in Context**

   Find the word *metabolized* in the passage. One definition below is closest to the meaning of that word. One definition has the opposite or nearly opposite meaning. The remaining definition has a completely different meaning. Label the definitions C for *closest,* O for *opposite or nearly opposite,* and D for *different.*

   _____ a. maintained

   _____ b. processed

   _____ c. cooled

2. **Distinguishing Fact from Opinion**

   Two of the statements below present *facts,* which can be proved correct. The other statement is an *opinion,* which expresses someone's thoughts or beliefs. Label the statements F for *fact* and O for *opinion.*

   _____ a. Starch is of great economic importance.

   _____ b. Starch is white, odorless, and tasteless.

   _____ c. Plants can convert starch into glucose.

3. Keeping Events in Order

Label the statements below 1, 2, and 3 to show the order in which the steps should be completed.

_____ a. Place a few drops of potassium iodide on the plant leaf.

_____ b. Place a leaf in alcohol and heat it for 10 minutes.

_____ c. Determine the amount of starch by judging the darkness of the color.

4. Making Correct Inferences

Two of the statements below are correct *inferences,* or reasonable guesses. They are based on information in the passage. The other statement is an incorrect, or faulty, inference. Label the statements C for *correct* inference and F for *faulty* inference.

_____ a. Starch and glucose have similar chemical properties.

_____ b. Potassium iodide reacts chemically with starch.

_____ c. The procedure described is the most exact method for determining the amount of starch in a plant.

5. Understanding Main Ideas

One of the statements below expresses the main idea of the passage. One statement is too general, or too broad. The other explains only part of the passage; it is too narrow. Label the statements M for *main idea,* B for *too broad,* and N for *too narrow.*

_____ a. A leaf should be put in heated alcohol before testing for starch.

_____ b. A potassium iodide solution can reveal a leaf's starch content.

_____ c. Plants store energy in the form of starch.

Correct Answers, Part A _____

Correct Answers, Part B _____

Total Correct Answers _____

People rarely feel as helpless as they do when confronted by the threat of severe storms. There is nothing that can prevent a hurricane, tornado, or major blizzard from causing devastation if it reaches a populated area. History offers numerous examples of storms that have destroyed large numbers of homes and killed many people. But today things are not as bleak as they were in the past. By studying the conditions that create storms, meteorologists are better able to predict them and give people in their paths the advance warning needed to avert tragedy.

A storm is defined as a sudden, extreme change in the normal conditions of Earth's atmosphere. Examples include a large influx of moisture or a sharp increase in wind velocity. These types of changes are generally caused by a dramatic shift in air pressure. In fact, air pressure often affects weather more than any other variable.

Air pressure and wind are intrinsically related. Wind is simply a movement of air from areas of high pressure to areas of lower pressure. Differences in pressure are caused by differences in heat energy within the atmosphere. Thus, a rapid increase in temperature within a particular area can cause pressure to decrease rapidly. For instance, a hurricane can form when a mass of cool air moves over warm ocean waters near the equator. As the air warms, it begins to ascend, with cool air rushing in to fill the void. As the cool air moves in, it begins to spin because of Earth's rotation. If the spinning winds reach velocities of 61 kilometers per hour (38 miles per hour), the storm is called a tropical storm. If winds reach 119 kilometers per hour (74 miles per hour), the storm is called a hurricane or typhoon.

Hurricanes are somewhat similar to tornadoes because both generate atmospheric vortices. A vortex is a cone-shaped depression of high-speed winds that can cause a great deal of destruction if it touches the ground. Because hurricanes require moisture to exist, they quickly expire over land. Unfortunately, when a hurricane comes to shore, it brings not only fierce winds but also large amounts of ocean water called storm surges. As the hurricane dies, it creates large thunderclouds that can cause heavy rain, thunder, lightning, and flooding. Tornadoes can also form from the breakup of hurricanes and are often one of their most dangerous consequences.

Reading Time _____

Recalling Facts

1. A sudden change in the conditions of Earth's atmosphere is called a
   - ❏ a. storm.
   - ❏ b. front.
   - ❏ c. pressure gradient.

2. Wind and _____ are closely related.
   - ❏ a. clouds
   - ❏ b. air pressure
   - ❏ c. thunder

3. A vortex is shaped like a
   - ❏ a. box.
   - ❏ b. cone.
   - ❏ c. sphere.

4. Differences in air pressure are caused mainly by differences in the _____ of areas of the atmosphere.
   - ❏ a. composition
   - ❏ b. moisture
   - ❏ c. temperature

5. Ocean water that is blown in by a hurricane is called a
   - ❏ a. tidal wave.
   - ❏ b. storm surge.
   - ❏ c. marine flood.

Understanding Ideas

6. You can infer that the reason there are fewer storm-related deaths than in the past is
   - ❏ a. weather forecasts are more accurate.
   - ❏ b. people are more careful.
   - ❏ c. people are healthier.

7. One can conclude from the article that hurricanes _____ begin in cold northern regions.
   - ❏ a. often
   - ❏ b. never
   - ❏ c. sometimes

8. If a major vortex existed over the Midwest, it would most likely be a
   - ❏ a. hurricane.
   - ❏ b. tornado.
   - ❏ c. typhoon.

9. Which of the following would be most likely to cause a storm?
   - ❏ a. a thick band of white clouds moving slowly across the sky
   - ❏ b. a mass of cool air moving into a warm area
   - ❏ c. a mass of warm air staying in the same place

10. The most likely result of a hurricane hitting a coastal area would be
    - ❏ a. thunderstorms.
    - ❏ b. an increase in atmospheric pressure.
    - ❏ c. a decrease in the likelihood of another hurricane during the next hurricane season.

What Is the Eye of a Hurricane?

The phenomenon known as the eye of a hurricane has always intrigued people. A hurricane is a massively destructive storm. Yet within the hurricane, one can find a relatively calm region—the eye—in which winds are eerily still and the sky surprisingly clear. Sometimes people make the mistake of thinking a hurricane has passed when they are actually in the eye of the storm.

A hurricane is a system of high-velocity winds and moisture that rotates in a counterclockwise direction. Hurricane formation is well understood; it is created by a rising system of temperate air. As the air rises, cooler air from the surrounding area moves in from all directions. Earth's rotation causes the air to begin swirling, pulling up ocean water along with the air.

Most scientists think the eye of a hurricane is simply the result of the normal conditions within a vortex, or circular system of wind. All twisting wind systems, whether hurricanes or dust devils, have the same vortex shape and similar characteristics. Just as strange as the calmness of the eye is the ferocity of the winds in the area surrounding the eye, called the eye wall. The heaviest rain, the strongest winds, and the worst pressure turbulence of the entire hurricane are located within the eye wall.

1. **Recognizing Words in Context**

   Find the word *temperate* in the passage. One definition below is closest to the meaning of that word. One definition has the opposite or nearly opposite meaning. The remaining definition has a completely different meaning. Label the definitions C for *closest,* O for *opposite or nearly opposite,* and D for *different.*

   _____ a. severe

   _____ b. measurable

   _____ c. mild

2. **Distinguishing Fact from Opinion**

   Two of the statements below present *facts,* which can be proved correct. The other statement is an *opinion,* which expresses someone's thoughts or beliefs. Label the statements F for *fact* and O for *opinion.*

   _____ a. A hurricane is formed by a system of rising warm air.

   _____ b. The area surrounding the hurricane eye is called the eye wall.

   _____ c. Hurricanes are the most dangerous kind of storm.

3. Keeping Events in Order

Label the statements below 1, 2, and 3 to show the order in which the events happen.

_____ a. A mass of warm air over the ocean begins to rise.

_____ b. The eye of the hurricane passes over a Caribbean island.

_____ c. The air begins to swirl.

4. Making Correct Inferences

Two of the statements below are correct *inferences,* or reasonable guesses. They are based on information in the passage. The other statement is an incorrect, or faulty, inference. Label the statements C for *correct* inference and F for *faulty* inference.

_____ a. Hurricanes winds are usually stronger than tornado winds.

_____ b. It is difficult for scientists to collect data concerning eye walls.

_____ c. Not all vortex systems have the same strength.

5. Understanding Main Ideas

One of the statements below expresses the main idea of the passage. One statement is too general, or too broad. The other explains only part of the passage; it is too narrow. Label the statements M for *main idea,* B for *too broad,* and N for *too narrow.*

_____ a. The different sections of a hurricane have very different characteristics.

_____ b. The eye of a hurricane is strikingly different from the rest of the storm.

_____ c. A hurricane rotates counterclockwise.

Correct Answers, Part A _____

Correct Answers, Part B _____

Total Correct Answers _____

Simple and Compound Machines

Human beings have always used tools; the ability to use and design tools for specific purposes and to fit particular needs is one characteristic that distinguishes humans from most other animals. Tools make people's lives easier by allowing them to complete tasks that might otherwise be difficult or impossible.

A machine is defined as a tool that reduces the amount of energy a person must expend in doing work. Machines play a part in virtually every aspect of a person's life; they can range in complexity from a hammer to a car engine.

Machines can be either simple or compound. A simple machine is a device with only one type of movement. For example, the pull tab on a soda can is a simple machine called a lever. Although this may appear to be a very simple machine, it would be difficult to break the seal and open the can without it. Even the cap on a bottled drink is a type of simple machine called a screw.

Other simple machines include the inclined plane, the wedge, the pulley, the wheel and axle, and the gear. An inclined plane is simply a sloping surface, such as a ramp. Screws and wedges are types of simple machines that allow only one kind of movement. They can be used to puncture or split hard solids such as wood. A pulley is a grooved wheel fitted with a chain, rope, or cord that glides along the grooved surface and can be used to raise flags or elevate window blinds. Yet another example of a simple machine is a wheel-and-axle mechanism, which consists of a rod that is attached to the center of a wheel. Examples of machines that incorporate wheel-and-axle mechanisms are doorknobs and faucets.

Compound machines are a combination of simple machines. These can be either basic or complicated in their design. For example, an ax is a basic compound machine that is composed of two simple machines: a lever and a wedge. A wheelbarrow is a compound machine that consists of a wheel and axle plus two levers.

More complicated compound machines include pencil sharpeners, airplanes, lawnmowers, and bicycles. Bicycles are compound machines composed of several simple machines that are easily recognized. The pedal apparatus combines levers with a wheel-and-axle system, gears transmit the pedals' motion to the rear wheel, the brakes are levers, and all the parts are fastened together with screws.

Reading Time _____

Recalling Facts

1. _____ is the term used for a tool that makes work easier by reducing the energy needed to complete a task.
   - ❏ a. An implement
   - ❏ b. A machine
   - ❏ c. A system

2. A ramp is an example of
   - ❏ a. an inclined plane.
   - ❏ b. a wedge.
   - ❏ c. a pulley.

3. Machines with only one type of movement are
   - ❏ a. complex machines.
   - ❏ b. compound machines.
   - ❏ c. simple machines.

4. An ax is an example of
   - ❏ a. a compound machine.
   - ❏ b. an outdated tool.
   - ❏ c. a simple machine.

5. A bicycle brake is a type of
   - ❏ a. lever.
   - ❏ b. screw.
   - ❏ c. pulley.

Understanding Ideas

6. An electric can opener includes a combination of a
   - ❏ a. pulley and a gear.
   - ❏ b. wheel-and-axle and a wedge.
   - ❏ c. screw and an ax.

7. A lever works by
   - ❏ a. allowing an object to be gradually moved upward.
   - ❏ b. transferring force from one end of an object to another.
   - ❏ c. turning in a circular motion.

8. In a pulley system, pulling down on a rope causes an object to
   - ❏ a. cut through another material.
   - ❏ b. pivot.
   - ❏ c. rise.

9. If turning the handle on a machine causes the machine to cut another object, then the machine is a
   - ❏ a. simple machine.
   - ❏ b. wheel-and-axle.
   - ❏ c. compound machine.

10. Which of the following would *not* be considered a machine?
    - ❏ a. shovel
    - ❏ b. paper
    - ❏ c. seesaw

Human-Powered Flying Machines

A compound machine that has received quite a lot of interest is a human-powered flying machine designed by engineers at the Massachusetts Institute of Technology during the 1980s. This machine, named *Daedalus*, has a rather simple but aerodynamically effective design.

Daedalus has pedals similar to those found on a bicycle. The plane is designed so that turning the pedals transfers their applied force to propellers. This is accomplished via the gears, similar to the way a bicycle's gears transfer the force of the pedals to the wheels. On *Daedalus*, the gear action causes the propellers to spin and the plane to fly a few meters above the ground.

To test *Daedalus*, the engineers used a Greek cycling champion named Kanellos Kanellopoulos. His challenge was to fly 115 kilometers (71 miles) from the Greek island of Crete to the island of Santorini. The pilot provides the only source of power for *Daedalus*. Therefore, the success of the mission would rely on the cyclist's stamina.

To accomplish this difficult endeavor, Kanellopoulos trained by pedaling nearly four hours a day. A strong wind arose near the end of his voyage and knocked a part of the tail off *Daedalus*, crashing the plane barely short of its goal of the shore of Santorini. Nevertheless, *Daedalus* set a distance record for a human-powered flying machine.

1. **Recognizing Words in Context**

   Find the word *stamina* in the passage. One definition below is closest to the meaning of that word. One definition has the opposite or nearly opposite meaning. The remaining definition has a completely different meaning. Label the definitions C for *closest*, O for *opposite or nearly opposite*, and D for *different*.

   _____ a. weakness

   _____ b. endurance

   _____ c. determination

2. **Distinguishing Fact from Opinion**

   Two of the statements below present *facts*, which can be proved correct. The other statement is an *opinion*, which expresses someone's thoughts or beliefs. Label the statements F for *fact* and O for *opinion*.

   _____ a. *Daedalus* is an ingenious human-powered flying machine.

   _____ b. There has been renewed interest in human–powered flying machines.

   _____ c. A Greek cycling champion piloted *Daedalus*.

3. Keeping Events in Order

Label the statements below 1, 2, and 3 to show the order in which the events happened.

_____ a. Kanellos Kanellopoulos pedaled for nearly four hours a day.

_____ b. *Daedalus* set a distance record.

_____ c. Engineers designed the human-powered flying machine *Daedalus*.

4. Making Correct Inferences

Two of the statements below are correct *inferences*, or reasonable guesses. They are based on information in the passage. The other statement is an incorrect, or faulty, inference. Label the statements C for *correct* inference and F for *faulty* inference.

_____ a. The *Daedalus* mission was a failure because it did not reach the shore of Santorini.

_____ b. *Daedalus* was designed to be lightweight.

_____ c. It is easier to use the legs rather than the arms to power a flying machine.

5. Understanding Main Ideas

One of the statements below expresses the main idea of the passage. One statement is too general, or too broad. The other explains only part of the passage; it is too narrow. Label the statements M for *main idea*, B for *too broad*, and N for *too narrow*.

_____ a. *Daedalus* was designed at the Massachusetts Institute of Technology.

_____ b. Compound machines are combinations of various simple machines.

_____ c. *Daedalus* is a compound machine that flies using only the power of its human operator.

Correct Answers, Part A _____

Correct Answers, Part B _____

Total Correct Answers _____

Human Diseases

A human disease is a condition that prevents the human body from functioning normally. Diseases are typically grouped into one of two classes: communicable and noncommunicable. When a disease is communicable, it can be spread from person to person; noncommunicable disease cannot be spread by human interaction. Both types of disease can be deadly. Yet communicable diseases more often are acute, meaning the symptoms appear quickly and intensify. In contrast, noncommunicable diseases tend to be chronic, or long-term, diseases that may remain dormant for many years but then appear suddenly and linger until death.

Communicable diseases are caused by bacteria, viruses, and parasites, all of which are capable of multiplying within a person and then spreading to other persons. Most people are familiar with communicable diseases because they have often been infected with them. For instance, one of the most common communicable diseases is a cold. The average person gets four colds a year through contact with other people. Other communicable diseases include meningitis, tuberculosis, and strep throat. When a person contracts one of these diseases, the incubation period—the time between exposure and the onset of symptoms—is typically between 12 and 24 hours. As a rule, if the disease is not too severe, the person recovers rather quickly. But if it is acute and the immune system is not able to suppress it, death can result.

Noncommunicable diseases differ from communicable disease in other ways. The most notable difference is the presence of a genetic link. Typically, people contract noncommunicable diseases not because they were exposed to some foreign agent such as a virus but because their genes somehow made them vulnerable. An example of genetically linked disease is cancer. Although it is not a certainty that people possessing so-called cancer genes will contract cancer, they are more likely to get the disease than the average person. This tendency suggests that some unknown agent activates cancer genes and triggers cancer cells to start growing.

Neuromuscular disorders are another type of disease with genetic links. These include multiple sclerosis and muscular dystrophy. In each of these, symptoms are mild at first but progressively worsen until finally the patient loses nearly all mobility.

Although doctors have many methods and medications at their disposal for treating disease, correct diagnosis can be difficult. Many symptoms are common to multiple diseases, and these symptoms appear in varying intensities in different victims.

Reading Time _____

Recalling Facts

1. Disease is a condition that prevents a person from
   - ❏ a. working.
   - ❏ b. functioning normally.
   - ❏ c. engaging in strenuous activities.

2. Diseases spread through human-to-human interactions are described as
   - ❏ a. communicable.
   - ❏ b. symptomatic.
   - ❏ c. noncommunicable.

3. Noncommunicable diseases include all the following *except*
   - ❏ a. cancer.
   - ❏ b. influenza.
   - ❏ c. multiple sclerosis.

4. The time between exposure to a disease-causing bacteria or virus and the onset of symptoms is called the
   - ❏ a. refractory period.
   - ❏ b. lag period.
   - ❏ c. incubation period.

5. A cold is a prevalent type of
   - ❏ a. noncommunicable disease.
   - ❏ b. fatal disease.
   - ❏ c. communicable disease.

Understanding Ideas

6. From the article, you can infer that when someone begins to display cold symptoms, they were probably exposed to the virus
   - ❏ a. 3 to 6 hours earlier.
   - ❏ b. 12 to 24 hours earlier.
   - ❏ c. several days earlier.

7. It can be inferred that a person who suffers from a serious neuromuscular disease will most likely
   - ❏ a. spread the disease to a family member.
   - ❏ b. get cancer also.
   - ❏ c. eventually lose most of his or her mobility.

8. The article suggests that symptoms of disease
   - ❏ a. can often appear quite mild.
   - ❏ b. are usually apparent right from the beginning.
   - ❏ c. occur quite predictably in all cases.

9. Which of the following natural events provides the best analogy to what happens when "cancer genes" are activated?
   - ❏ a. a steady rain
   - ❏ b. an avalanche
   - ❏ c. a tornado

10. One can reasonably assume that in the future scientists will find
   - ❏ a. a cure for every disease.
   - ❏ b. genetic links to many other diseases.
   - ❏ c. twice as many communicable diseases.

7 B   Allergens

The human immune system is responsible for destroying foreign substances that enter the body. These can be harmful substances, such as bacteria or viruses, or mostly benign substances, such as dust. But sometimes the immune system can overreact. When the body responds strongly to a fairly harmless foreign substance, a person may suffer from a variety of symptoms that together are known as an allergy. The causative agent of the allergy is called an allergen.

Allergens vary from person to person because different people are sensitive to different substances. For example, many people are allergic to dust mites, which are common in household bedding. A person who is sensitive to dust mites may wake up in the morning with a sore throat and stuffy nose, although dust mites do not bother other people at all.

Other common allergens include pet hair, skin particles, and leaf mold. When a person who is allergic to dog hair goes into a place where a dog has been, he or she may immediately begin wheezing due to the dilation of blood vessels and the contraction of the smooth-muscle tissue in their respiratory tract. Watering of the eyes and sneezing are other common allergic reactions. Once the person leaves the place, he or she may once again feel perfectly fine until being exposed to the problematic allergen again.

1. **Recognizing Words in Context**

   Find the word *benign* in the passage. One definition below is closest to the meaning of that word. One definition has the opposite or nearly opposite meaning. The remaining definition has a completely different meaning. Label the definitions C for *closest,* O for *opposite or nearly opposite,* and D for *different.*

   _____ a. harmless

   _____ b. inquisitive

   _____ c. dangerous

2. **Distinguishing Fact from Opinion**

   Two of the statements below present *facts,* which can be proved correct. The other statement is an *opinion,* which expresses someone's thoughts or beliefs. Label the statements F for *fact* and O for *opinion.*

   _____ a. The causative agent of an allergy is called an allergen.

   _____ b. Allergies can cause a variety of symptoms.

   _____ c. The human immune system should function better than it does.

3. **Keeping Events in Order**

Label the statements below 1, 2, and 3 to show the order in which the events happen.

_____ a. A person encounters an allergen.

_____ b. The allergen is removed and the person begins to feel better.

_____ c. A variety of allergy-related symptoms begin.

4. **Making Correct Inferences**

Two of the statements below are correct *inferences,* or reasonable guesses. They are based on information in the passage. The other statement is an incorrect, or faulty, inference. Label the statements C for *correct* inference and F for *faulty* inference.

_____ a. Allergens can exist in people's homes without their knowledge.

_____ b. Although not everyone is allergic to pets, everyone has some type of allergy.

_____ c. People with the same allergies may not have the same sets of symptoms.

5. **Understanding Main Ideas**

One of the statements below expresses the main idea of the passage. One statement is too general, or too broad. The other explains only part of the passage; it is too narrow. Label the statements M for *main idea,* B for *too broad,* and N for *too narrow.*

_____ a. The human immune system functions well in some situations and not as well in others.

_____ b. The dust mite is a common household allergen.

_____ c. Allergens are relatively harmless substances that trigger strong immune reactions in some people.

Correct Answers, Part A _____

Correct Answers, Part B _____

Total Correct Answers _____

8   A   The Beliefs of Aristotle

Aristotle, philosopher and scientist, is considered one of the greatest thinkers in history. He was born in 384 B.C. in northern Greece. He studied under another brilliant and influential man named Plato. Aristotle not only studied philosophy and science; he also mastered many other subjects, such as politics, psychology, and rhetoric. His thirst for knowledge and for some sort of divine truth or logic set him apart from most of his contemporaries. In fact, many of his ideas concerning philosophy were so profound that they have challenged philosophical minds ever since and continue to be influential today.

One of Aristotle's greatest achievements was in pioneering the study of zoology. This field allowed him to use perhaps his most formidable skill— observation. Unlike many other ancient thinkers, Aristotle was a meticulous observer and recorder of natural phenomena. Over time, Aristotle classified more than 500 animal species in hierarchies based on biological traits. Carolus Linnaeus further developed this type of classification system some 2,100 years later.

An interesting aspect of Aristotle's brilliance was that many of his ideas were very different from those of other thinkers and thus not always popular. For instance, he studied the behavior and features of many marine species; included was a detailed study of dolphins. Aristotle noticed that a pregnant dolphin nourished her fetus through an organ called a placenta and gave birth to live young, as land-dwelling mammals do. Therefore, he grouped dolphins with mammals instead of with fish species as other ancient biologists had. Despite the accuracy of his grouping, his successors classified dolphins as fish, and it took 2,000 years for scientists to reclassify them as mammals.

Not all of Aristotle's theories proved to be accurate, however. In astronomy, for example, Aristotle was heavily influenced by the religious teachings of his day. As Aristotle watched the night skies, he concluded that Earth was the center of the universe and the Sun and the other planets revolved around it. This theory is known as the geocentric model of the universe. Later it was discovered that all the planets in fact revolve around the Sun. This theory is known as the heliocentric model. To Aristotle and others, however, Earth was the perfect creation of a higher order. The ancient Greeks were unwilling to accept that such a perfect creation could move. In their philosophy, anything that moved or changed was seen as unstable and thus flawed.

Reading Time _____

Recalling Facts

1. Aristotle was
   - ❑ a. a Roman.
   - ❑ b. a Greek.
   - ❑ c. an Egyptian.

2 Aristotle developed a classification system for
   - ❑ a. rocks.
   - ❑ b. animals.
   - ❑ c. plants.

3. Aristotle differed from his contemporaries in that he wanted to find some sort of
   - ❑ a. mathematical model.
   - ❑ b. divine logic.
   - ❑ c. military superiority.

4. Dolphins are most accurately categorized as
   - ❑ a. marine reptiles.
   - ❑ b. fish.
   - ❑ c. mammals.

5. Aristotle's teachings in _____ are still influential today.
   - ❑ a. philosophy
   - ❑ b. zoology
   - ❑ c. fine art

Understanding Ideas

6. According to the article, Aristotle differed from many biologists of his day because he
   - ❑ a. studied the anatomy of many different species.
   - ❑ b. excelled in observation.
   - ❑ c. kept records of different species for multiple generations.

7. You can infer that the _____ model of the universe has been shown to be the correct one.
   - ❑ a. Aristotelian
   - ❑ b. heliocentric
   - ❑ c. geocentric

8. You can infer that one of the reasons Aristotle is still highly respected in modern times is
   - ❑ a. he introduced important ideas in so many different areas.
   - ❑ b. he created the civilization known as ancient Greece.
   - ❑ c. his descriptions of the universe contributed to the development of the space program.

9. Which would *not* have contributed to the ancient Greeks' belief in a geocentric universe?
   - ❑ a. their inability to feel Earth moving through its orbit
   - ❑ b. the pattern in which solar and lunar eclipses occur
   - ❑ c. the rising and setting of the Sun

10. You can infer that college students today are most likely to study Aristotle's views on
    - ❑ a. zoology.
    - ❑ b. psychology.
    - ❑ c. philosophy.

Nicolaus Copernicus and His Heliocentric Model

The development of astronomy was heavily influenced by the ideas of the ancient Greeks. Aristotle believed that Earth was the center of the universe and the Sun and other planets rotated around it. This geocentric model was refined by another Greek, Ptolemy, and accepted as truth for more than 1,000 years. It was then that the development of mathematical models and of precise instruments allowed scientists to put Earth in its proper place.

The first scientist to mount an effective challenge to the Ptolemaic model was the Polish scholar Nicolaus Copernicus. From his calculations of the movements of heavenly bodies, he developed, in the early 1500s, a model of the universe in which the planets revolved around the Sun. This heliocentric model was given credence by only a handful of scientists, because the theories of Aristotle were then so popular that few people were willing to accept any other explanation.

Copernicus's heliocentric theory began to gain wider acceptance as a result of the work of Galileo Galilei in the 1600s. Using a newly invented device called the telescope, Galileo was able to study the solar system more closely than anyone before had been. Galileo proclaimed Copernicus's theory to be correct. This challenged the deeply held beliefs of authorities in his native Italy. Although threatened by the authorities, Galileo published his results and spent the last years of his life under house arrest.

1. **Recognizing Words in Context**

   Find the word *credence* in the passage. One definition below is closest to the meaning of that word. One definition has the opposite or nearly opposite meaning. The remaining definition has a completely different meaning. Label the definitions C for *closest*, O for *opposite or nearly opposite*, and D for *different*.

   _____ a. rejection

   _____ b. publication

   _____ c. acceptance

2. **Distinguishing Fact from Opinion**

   Two of the statements below present *facts*, which can be proved correct. The other statement is an *opinion*, which expresses someone's thoughts or beliefs. Label the statements F for *fact* and O for *opinion*.

   _____ a. The ancient Greeks developed a geocentric model of the universe.

   _____ b. Galileo did important work using telescopes.

   _____ c. The heliocentric model of the universe would not have been proved without the telescope.

3. **Keeping Events in Order**

   Label the statements below 1, 2, and 3 to show the order in which the events happened.

   _____ a. Nicolaus Copernicus developed his model of the universe.

   _____ b. Galileo used a telescope to study the night sky.

   _____ c. The heliocentric model of the universe became widely accepted.

4. **Making Correct Inferences**

   Two of the statements below are correct *inferences,* or reasonable guesses. They are based on information in the passage. The other statement is an incorrect, or faulty, inference. Label the statements C for *correct* inference and F for *faulty* inference.

   _____ a. Galileo helped to popularize the theories of Copernicus.

   _____ b. All of Aristotle's ideas about the universe were wrong.

   _____ c. Copernicus did not have a telescope.

5. **Understanding Main Ideas**

   One of the statements below expresses the main idea of the passage. One statement is too general, or too broad. The other explains only part of the passage; it is too narrow. Label the statements M for *main idea,* B for *too broad,* and N for *too narrow.*

   _____ a. Throughout history, new scientific ideas have replaced older ones.

   _____ b. Ptolemy refined Aristotle's geocentric model of the universe.

   _____ c. Copernicus's heliocentric model replaced the Greeks' geocentric model.

   Correct Answers, Part A _____

   Correct Answers, Part B _____

   Total Correct Answers _____

Blood and the Circulatory System

The human heart is constantly at work. The average heart beats about 100,000 times per day and pumps 4.7 liters (5 quarts) of blood per minute through the entire body. As it beats, the heart relies on numerous vessels and organs to help distribute the blood. Blood delivers vital nutrients and oxygen. It also picks up waste materials and drops them off at organs specifically designed to dispose of waste. Thus, the bloodstream and blood vessels are like an intricate conveyor-belt system that picks up, carries, and delivers packages throughout a huge building, with the heart acting as the motor that keeps the system running. Blood, blood vessels, and the heart work together to help every part of the body get what it needs and get rid of what it doesn't need.

Because the heart is composed of cardiac muscle, it never tires. Cardiac muscle consists of special cells that allow it to contract strongly and in precise rhythms. Layers of these cells form the tissue that is wrapped around the chambers of the heart. When the tissue contracts, it forces blood out of the chambers.

The heartbeat begins when an electrical impulse spreads from the top of the heart to the bottom. The impulse passes quickly through the upper portion but slows somewhat through the less conductive bottom portion. The sequential contraction and relaxation of the heart creates the familiar two-part heartbeat.

As blood is pumped from the heart, it begins a journey that takes it through the equivalent of 97,000 kilometers (60,000 miles) of blood vessels. The journey begins with the arteries that carry the blood away from the heart. The blood travels through the arteries to areas that are farther and farther from the heart. The arteries become progressively smaller as they get farther from the heart; the very smallest arteries are called arterioles. The arterioles lead to networks of microscopic blood vessels called capillaries. Capillaries are so thin that red blood cells can flow through them only in single file.

Gas exchange occurs through the walls of the capillaries. The blood delivers oxygen to the body's tissues and picks up carbon dioxide, a waste product of cell activity. The now oxygen-poor blood, called deoxygenated blood, is pumped back to the heart through the veins and then to the lungs. There the body can dispose of the carbon dioxide through exhalation and pick up more oxygen through inhalation.

Reading Time _____

Recalling Facts

1. Arteries carry blood
   - ❑ a. away from the heart.
   - ❑ b. toward the heart.
   - ❑ c. to the brain only.

2. The heartbeat is a _____ sequence.
   - ❑ a. three-part
   - ❑ b. two-part
   - ❑ c. five-part

3. The smallest blood vessels are called
   - ❑ a. arteries.
   - ❑ b. capillaries.
   - ❑ c. arterioles.

4. Oxygen-poor blood is also known as
   - ❑ a. oxygenated blood.
   - ❑ b. deoxygenated blood.
   - ❑ c. nutrient-rich blood.

5. A main type of waste product removed by the blood is
   - ❑ a. nitrogen.
   - ❑ b. oxygen.
   - ❑ c. carbon dioxide.

Understanding Ideas

6. According to the article, one of the most important functions of the heart is to
   - ❑ a. serve as the emotional center of the body.
   - ❑ b. make red blood cells.
   - ❑ c. help blood reach distant regions of the body.

7. From the information in the article, one could conclude that
   - ❑ a. force is required to move fluid through a conduit.
   - ❑ b. the heart beats the same number of times a day for everyone.
   - ❑ c. the heart would function more efficiently if it were composed of skeletal muscle.

8. The types of blood vessel at the tip of a finger are most likely
   - ❑ a. arteries.
   - ❑ b. capillaries.
   - ❑ c. veins.

9. If the blood in arterioles is a brighter red than the blood in veins, one can infer that
   - ❑ a. oxygen-rich blood has the brighter color.
   - ❑ b. oxygen-poor blood has the brighter color.
   - ❑ c. veins have walls that absorb color.

10. From the article, one can infer that the primary function of the bloodstream is
    - ❑ a. transportation.
    - ❑ b. inhalation.
    - ❑ c. transmittal of nerve impulses.

Sickle-cell anemia is a genetic disease that originated thousands of years ago in parts of Africa, Europe, and Asia. The disease spread as people migrated; it currently affects millions of people in many parts of the world, chiefly Africa and the Mediterranean. It is caused by flawed hemoglobin that triggers red blood cells to change shape once they release oxygen. Hemoglobin is an iron-carrying pigment that assists in oxygen transport.

Normal red blood cells have a fixed, doughnutlike shape that allows them to flow smoothly through the blood vessels, including the capillaries. In contrast, when the red blood cells of a person with sickle-cell anemia release oxygen, they can develop a crescent shape similar to that of a sickle, a tool that is used to cut grain. The crescent-shaped cells clump together and block the flow of blood. Eventually the blood is unable to reach certain regions of the body, which leads to pain and tissue damage. In addition, sickle cells die quickly, so sickle-cell patients are chronically deficient in red blood cells, resulting in the condition known as anemia.

There is no known cure for sickle-cell anemia. Doctors try to manage the symptoms by prescribing supplements of folic acid, which helps in the generation of new red blood cells. Patients are advised to avoid dehydration and to rest when symptoms are acute.

1. **Recognizing Words in Context**

   Find the word *chronically* in the passage. One definition below is closest to the meaning of that word. One definition has the opposite or nearly opposite meaning. The remaining definition has a completely different meaning. Label the definitions C for *closest*, O for *opposite or nearly opposite*, and D for *different*.

   _____ a. never

   _____ b. continually

   _____ c. increasingly

2. **Distinguishing Fact from Opinion**

   Two of the statements below present *facts*, which can be proved correct. The other statement is an *opinion*, which expresses someone's thoughts or beliefs. Label the statements F for *fact* and O for *opinion*.

   _____ a. Hemoglobin assists in carrying oxygen to different parts of the body.

   _____ b. The red blood cells of sickle-cell anemia victims tend to clump together.

   _____ c. More attention needs to be given to finding treatments for sickle-cell anemia.

3. Keeping Events in Order

Two of the statements below describe events that happened at the same time. The other statement describes an event that happened before or after those events. Label them S for *same time*, B for *before*, or A for *after*.

_____ a. Red blood cells of a person with sickle-cell anemia released oxygen.

_____ b. Millions of red-blood cells blocked the flow of oxygen to a foot, causing damage to the foot's tissue.

_____ c. Red blood cells of a sickle-cell patient changed shape.

4. Making Correct Inferences

Two of the statements below are correct *inferences,* or reasonable guesses. They are based on information in the passage. The other statement is an incorrect, or faulty, inference. Label the statements C for *correct* inference and F for *faulty* inference.

_____ a. With today's advanced medical technology, doctors will soon find a cure for sickle-cell anemia.

_____ b. Sickle-cell anemia is a chronic, or lifelong, disease.

_____ c. Other health problems may aggravate sickle-cell anemia.

5. Understanding Main Ideas

One of the statements below expresses the main idea of the passage. One statement is too general, or too broad. The other explains only part of the passage; it is too narrow. Label the statements M for *main idea,* B for *too broad,* and N for *too narrow.*

_____ a. Normal red blood cells flow smoothly, whereas red blood cells of sickle-cell patients clump together.

_____ b. Sickle-cell anemia is an inherited blood disease causing a change in the shape and efficiency of red blood cells.

_____ c. The study of genetic diseases is a relatively new science.

Correct Answers, Part A _____

Correct Answers, Part B _____

Total Correct Answers _____

10 | A | Kinetic and Potential Energy

Virtually every process on Earth requires energy. For instance, people eat food to give their bodies energy. Energy in the form of light allows people to see, and energy in the form of heat keeps people warm. The transfer of energy from one form to another is the subject of some of the most basic laws of physics.

Energy exists in so many forms that it is difficult to define. A popular definition is that energy is the ability to cause change. Two examples of such energy are kinetic energy and potential energy. Other examples include chemical energy, or energy from atoms; thermal energy, or energy from heat; and radiant energy, or energy traveling in light.

Energy that results from motion is called kinetic energy. Any object that is experiencing some form of motion has some degree of kinetic energy. For example, a rolling ball, a flying boomerang, and an accelerating car all have kinetic energy. These moving objects have different amounts of kinetic energy. The larger the object is and the faster it moves, the greater its kinetic energy. In other words, a truck traveling at 80 kilometers per hour has more kinetic energy than a dog running at 25 kilometers per hour.

A second type of energy is potential energy. Unlike kinetic energy, potential energy does not involve motion. Instead, potential energy can be thought of as stored energy that relates to the position of an object. This type of energy is called potential energy because the object has the potential to develop kinetic energy if specific conditions are met. It can thus be said that there is a fundamental relationship between kinetic energy and potential energy.

To better understand the relationship between kinetic energy and potential energy, picture a rock sitting on the edge of a cliff. The rock, although stationary, has the potential to fall and thus possesses potential energy. The higher the cliff, the farther the rock could potentially fall, and therefore the greater its potential energy. When the rock is on the edge of the cliff, it is at rest and so has no kinetic energy. If someone pushes the rock over the edge of the cliff, however, it will fall quickly toward the ground. As the rock falls, it gains kinetic energy. This gain in kinetic energy is equal to the amount of potential energy that the rock loses as it approaches the ground.

Reading Time _____

Recalling Facts

1. Energy is defined as the ability to cause
   - ❏ a. growth.
   - ❏ b. change.
   - ❏ c. rapid movement.

2. Energy from heat is called
   - ❏ a. thermal energy.
   - ❏ b. chemical energy.
   - ❏ c. mechanical energy.

3. A type of energy that does not involve motion is
   - ❏ a. kinetic energy.
   - ❏ b. potential energy.
   - ❏ c. mechanical energy.

4. Energy from motion is called
   - ❏ a. kinetic energy.
   - ❏ b. thermal energy.
   - ❏ c. potential energy.

5. A ball that is rolling downhill has
   - ❏ a. dynamic energy.
   - ❏ b. potential energy.
   - ❏ c. kinetic energy.

Understanding Ideas

6. According to the article, the higher an object is held above the ground, the greater its
   - ❏ a. potential energy.
   - ❏ b. gravitational inertia.
   - ❏ c. kinetic energy.

7. The engine of a car that is accelerating uphill possesses both
   - ❏ a. kinetic energy and potential energy.
   - ❏ b. radiant energy and kinetic energy.
   - ❏ c. potential energy and radiant energy.

8. From the article, one can infer that one of the most important factors in assessing the amount of potential energy in an object is the
   - ❏ a. shape of the object.
   - ❏ b. position of the object.
   - ❏ c. history of the object.

9. It can be inferred from the article that
   - ❏ a. the total amount of energy on Earth is decreasing.
   - ❏ b. larger objects always have more kinetic energy than smaller objects.
   - ❏ c. some energy enters our atmosphere from the Sun.

10. Which of the following has the greatest kinetic energy?
    - ❏ a. A 200-gram ball traveling at 40 kilometers per hour.
    - ❏ b. A 200-gram ball traveling at 80 kilometers per hour.
    - ❏ c. A 100-gram ball traveling at 80 kilometers per hour.

Sports and Potential Energy

Sports provide examples of the conversion of potential energy to kinetic energy. Skiers, for example, use gravity to help them convert potential energy to kinetic energy when they glide down a slope. As they ride back up to the top of the slope in a ski lift, they gain potential energy. At the top of the slope, their potential energy is at a maximum. Once they lean forward, gravity takes control, and they speed down the slope toward the bottom. If the angle of the slope remains constant on their way down, their potential energy lessens in direct proportion to their gain in kinetic energy, meaning that their speed increases as they get closer to the bottom of the slope. This is why some skiers find it necessary to brake intermittently. Unless they slow their descent, they may reach a speed beyond their control.

Another sport that illustrates the relationship between potential and kinetic energy is trampolining. Here, the potential energy results from the tightly coiled springs that connect the elastic material of the trampoline bed to the metal frame. When a person jumps on a trampoline, the force stretches the springs, maximizing their potential energy. This energy is quickly converted into kinetic energy as the springs recoil, propelling the jumper into the air.

1. **Recognizing Words in Context**

   Find the word *intermittently* in the passage. One definition below is closest to the meaning of that word. One definition has the opposite or nearly opposite meaning. The remaining definition has a completely different meaning. Label the definitions C for *closest*, O for *opposite or nearly opposite*, and D for *different*.

   _____ a. unskillfully

   _____ b. occasionally

   _____ c. continuously

2. **Distinguishing Fact from Opinion**

   Two of the statements below present *facts*, which can be proved correct. The other statement is an *opinion*, which expresses someone's thoughts or beliefs. Label the statements F for *fact* and O for *opinion*.

   _____ a. A skier gliding down a mountain experiences a loss of potential energy.

   _____ b. Kinetic energy is more useful than potential energy.

   _____ c. Sometimes kinetic energy increases as potential energy decreases.

3. **Keeping Events in Order**

Label the statements below 1, 2, and 3 to show the order in which the events happen.

_____ a. A skier experiences a gain in kinetic energy.

_____ b. A skier approaches the top of a mountain.

_____ c. A skier reaches a maximum amount of potential energy.

4. **Making Correct Inferences**

Two of the statements below are correct *inferences,* or reasonable guesses. They are based on information in the passage. The other statement is an incorrect, or faulty, inference. Label the statements C for *correct* inference and F for *faulty* inference.

_____ a. Kinetic energy plays a bigger role in sports than potential energy does.

_____ b. The greater the amount of kinetic energy involved in a sport, the more popular it is.

_____ c. The higher a mountain is, the greater the potential energy of a skier at its top.

5. **Understanding Main Ideas**

One of the statements below expresses the main idea of the passage. One statement is too general, or too broad. The other explains only part of the passage; it is too narrow. Label the statements M for *main idea,* B for *too broad,* and N for *too narrow.*

_____ a. Sports provide examples of the laws of physics.

_____ b. Sports involve the conversion of potential energy to kinetic energy.

_____ c. A skier at the top of a hill has potential energy.

Correct Answers, Part A _____

Correct Answers, Part B _____

Total Correct Answers _____

The discovery of antibiotics forever changed the way disease is treated. These "wonder drugs" save millions of lives every year by killing or stopping the reproduction of potentially deadly bacteria. Diseases such as scarlet fever have been virtually wiped out in developed countries. Many fewer people die from infections today than 100 years ago. Still, despite these important gains, the future of this medical treatment is uncertain, due to the very nature of bacteria.

Bacteria are single-celled organisms that are too small to be seen with the naked eye. They reproduce by simple cell division; offspring are therefore usually genetically identical to their parent. Bacteria replicate very quickly, on average about once every 20 minutes. So, within the span of a few days, a small number of bacteria can grow to millions.

Bacteria are everywhere. Therefore, if a type of bacteria is harmful, it threatens and can affect a large number of people very quickly. For this reason, it is important to have a means to prevent bacteria from spreading and thereby stop disease from spreading.

Antibiotics work either by killing specific bacteria, called strains, or by slowing their growth. Alexander Fleming of Scotland discovered antibiotics in 1929 when he found that penicillium mold could stop bacteria from growing. This mold contains a compound called penicillin that stops the growth of bacteria by hindering their ability to build cell walls. This helps prevent the bacteria from reproducing and leaves them vulnerable to attack by the body's immune system.

After Fleming's initial discovery, biologists found many additional substances capable of destroying bacteria by stopping their cellular functions. Some are chemicals extracted from living things; others are developed in laboratories. Antibiotics are used to treat a wide variety of bacterial illnesses such as strep throat, infections of wounds, and pneumonia.

One problem that has arisen with antibiotics is that some bacteria are able to resist them. Whenever bacteria reproduce, some mutate. When an organism mutates, some of its genetic material is randomly rearranged during reproduction so that the offspring has one or more characteristics that are different from the parent organism's. If the bacteria mutate in such a way that the offspring are not affected by antibiotics, these offspring will survive and reproduce until all of the bacteria of a given population are resistant to antibiotics. For this reason, scientists are continuously working to develop new antibiotics that are effective against resistant bacteria.

Reading Time _____

Recalling Facts

1. Substances that destroy bacteria are called
   - ❏ a. antibiotics.
   - ❏ b. bacterial strains.
   - ❏ c. inhibitors.

2. The person responsible for discovering antibiotics was
   - ❏ a. Linus Pauling.
   - ❏ b. Alexander Fleming.
   - ❏ c. Niels Bohr.

3. An example of an antibiotic is
   - ❏ a. aspirin.
   - ❏ b. penicillin.
   - ❏ c. an antihistamine.

4. Antibiotics interfere with the _____ of bacteria.
   - ❏ a. ovulation
   - ❏ b. reproduction
   - ❏ c. respiration

5. Some antibiotics are derived from living things, while others
   - ❏ a. appear randomly in the atmosphere.
   - ❏ b. are obtained from metamorphic rock.
   - ❏ c. are produced in laboratories.

Understanding Ideas

6. One can conclude that bacteria
   - ❏ a. reproduce slowly.
   - ❏ b. are found only at locations that have unsanitary conditions.
   - ❏ c. are microscopic.

7. Which of the following statements is most likely true?
   - ❏ a. The potential of antibiotics is limitless.
   - ❏ b. Scientists are developing improved antibiotics.
   - ❏ c. If any antibiotic becomes ineffective, scientists will be able to replace it.

8. The article suggests that most of the offspring of antibiotic-resistant bacteria are also resistant because
   - ❏ a. they have genetic makeups that are similar to their parents'.
   - ❏ b. they learned how to seek out and attack antibiotics.
   - ❏ c. they contain cytotoxins that destroy antibiotics.

9. One can conclude that
   - ❏ a. antibiotics in use today will always be effective.
   - ❏ b. new treatments for bacterial disease may be necessary.
   - ❏ c. antibiotics are useless.

10. People in less-developed countries have probably not benefited from antibiotics as much as people in industrialized countries have because
    - ❏ a. antibiotics are less widely available in these regions.
    - ❏ b. people refuse to take them.
    - ❏ c. antibiotics are not effective in some parts of the world.

Antibiotic resistance occurs when bacteria become immune to a substance that is designed to kill them. Bacteria can become resistant to drugs quite easily. Their ability to do this relates to a driving force of nature known as survival of the fittest.

When bacteria reproduce, mutations produce a small number of bacteria that are resistant to antibiotics. An even smaller number of offspring are resistant to multiple antibiotics. These super-resistant bacteria will continue to reproduce as other strains die out. Eventually the super-resistant bacteria become the norm. If these bacteria are disease causing, they can pose a serious threat to human populations.

Improper use of antibiotics can contribute to the development of super-resistant bacteria. Antibiotics do not work on viral illnesses such as colds and flu. If people take antibiotics for such illnesses, the drugs will do nothing to make them feel better and will kill nonresistant bacteria unnecessarily. Resistant bacteria will not be killed, and they will take over the bacteria population.

Although the development of super-resistant bacteria is unfortunate from a medical standpoint, it is a remarkable process. By introducing antibiotics into bacteria populations, humans have accelerated bacterial evolution, creating bacteria that are more fit to survive attacks by their enemies, including antibiotics.

1. **Recognizing Words in Context**

   Find the word *norm* in the passage. One definition below is closest to the meaning of that word. One definition has the opposite or nearly opposite meaning. The remaining definition has a completely different meaning. Label the definitions C for *closest*, O for *opposite or nearly opposite,* and D for *different.*

   _____ a. strength

   _____ b. exception

   _____ c. standard

2. **Distinguishing Fact from Opinion**

   Two of the statements below present *facts,* which can be proved correct. The other statement is an *opinion,* which expresses someone's thoughts or beliefs. Label the statements F for *fact* and O for *opinion.*

   _____ a. Super-resistant bacteria are one of the greatest threats to human welfare.

   _____ b. Some bacteria have a natural immunity to certain antibiotics.

   _____ c. Antibiotics are drugs that kill harmful bacteria.

3. Keeping Events in Order

Label the statements below 1, 2, and 3 to show the order in which the events happen.

_____ a. Some doctors prescribe the antibiotic to large numbers of people.

_____ b. Eventually many bacteria become resistant.

_____ c. An antibiotic is developed to help cure a bacterial disease.

4. Making Correct Inferences

Two of the statements below are correct *inferences,* or reasonable guesses. They are based on information in the passage. The other statement is an incorrect, or faulty, inference. Label the statements C for *correct* inference and F for *faulty* inference.

_____ a. Reducing the inappropriate use of antibiotics would lessen the threat of super-resistant bacteria.

_____ b. All bacteria will eventually become antibiotic-resistant.

_____ c. Medical researchers are paying increasing attention to super-resistant bacteria.

5. Understanding Main Ideas

One of the statements below expresses the main idea of the passage. One statement is too general, or too broad. The other explains only part of the passage; it is too narrow. Label the statements M for *main idea*, B for *too broad*, and N for *too narrow*.

_____ a. Antibiotic resistance is a serious medical problem.

_____ b. Bacterial reproduction results in mutations.

_____ c. The study of bacteria continues to evolve as new information and new technology become available.

Correct Answers, Part A _____

Correct Answers, Part B _____

Total Correct Answers _____

How Substances Move Through Plants

Plants possess unique structures that enable them to efficiently transport water, nutrients, and waste to and from their many parts. Unlike animal cells, plant cells contain rigid outer layers called cell walls. Cell walls help to strengthen a plant's structure and minimize water loss. Although animal cells have semipermeable membranes, the cell walls of plants are nearly impermeable. Therefore, plant cells must rely on pathways called plasmodesmata to exchange materials. A plasmodesma passes through a cell wall without compromising the rigid structure that helps plants survive harsh environments.

Another important feature of a plant cell is the central vacuole. This structure stores water, essential chemicals, pigments, and waste. The vacuole is elastic in nature; it expands and shrinks in response to the amount of water it contains. Vacuoles are like reservoirs. Without vacuoles, plants would be unable to survive droughts.

Water and minerals enter plants through their roots. Roots have the ability to absorb such minerals as magnesium, potassium, calcium, and iron as needed. Roots can also screen out unnecessary or harmful materials, including toxins. Sources of minerals include bacteria, fungi, and fertilizer. Roots come in a variety of forms that vary with the needs of the plants. Some plants contain only one primary root, the taproot. Plants with taproots include radishes and carrots, in which the root itself is the part generally consumed for food by animals. Other plants have a fibrous root system, with numerous smaller roots extending from a larger trunk. This type of system is present in plants ranging from simple grasses to tall trees. Fibrous roots come into contact with a larger volume of soil than taproots do, allowing for absorption over a broader area.

Water and minerals move from the roots to other parts of the plant through tissue called xylem. Xylem consists of cells that are long, narrow, and hollow. Xylem cells are grouped together in columns. Much water must be brought from the roots up to the leaves, where it is needed for photosynthesis. Large amounts of water evaporate from the leaves of plants, which also release large amounts of oxygen into the atmosphere as the by-product of photosynthesis.

Phloem is the tissue that transports carbohydrates in plants. Leaves produce carbohydrates as a result of photosynthesis. The long phloem cells contain sievelike structures that allow only these carbohydrates to move from the leaves to other parts of the plant.

Reading Time _____

Recalling Facts

1. The rigid outer layer of a plant cell is called the
   - ❑ a. semipermeable membrane.
   - ❑ b. plasmodesma. .
   - ❑ c. cell wall.

2. The structure that stores water and waste in a plant cell is the
   - ❑ a. central vacuole.
   - ❑ b. plasmodesma.
   - ❑ c. phloem.

3. Roots benefit plants by doing all of the following *except*
   - ❑ a. screening out harmful substances.
   - ❑ b. protecting plants from harsh weather.
   - ❑ c. absorbing minerals.

4. The type of root structure in a carrot plant is a
   - ❑ a. taproot.
   - ❑ b. vascular root.
   - ❑ c. fibrous root.

5. The part of a plant that carries water and minerals upward from the roots is the
   - ❑ a. phloem.
   - ❑ b. central vacuole.
   - ❑ c. xylem.

Understanding Ideas

6. From the information in the article, one can infer that _____ are particularly responsible for helping plants to survive harsh conditions.
   - ❑ a. roots and leaves
   - ❑ b. cell walls and central vacuoles
   - ❑ c. xylem and phloem

7. One can infer from the article that plants get zinc through their
   - ❑ a. roots.
   - ❑ b. leaves.
   - ❑ c. phloem.

8. The most likely result of a plant's experiencing several days without rain would be
   - ❑ a. a swelling of its central vacuoles.
   - ❑ b. a shrinking of its central vacuoles.
   - ❑ c. its certain death.

9. If you know that different kinds of sugars travel through phloem, you can infer that sugars
   - ❑ a. are absorbed by roots.
   - ❑ b. are carbohydrates.
   - ❑ c. are not involved in photosynthesis.

10. Which of the following statements is most likely true?
    - ❑ a. Plants with one central root structure often receive fewer nutrients than they need.
    - ❑ b. Soil that is not treated with artificial fertilizer always lacks some essential nutrients.
    - ❑ c. Plants have evolved root systems according to their nutritional needs.

Plant Pigments

Nature is full of vibrant colors. Plants exhibit almost all colors imaginable. Their variety of colors is due to pigments, chemical compounds that reflect light in different ways. The type of pigments in a plant depends on the plant's genetic characteristics. To understand how color is created, scientists are looking at the ways in which plant genes are coded for color.

Plant geneticists have been trying to discover the mystery behind plant pigments for some time, but only recently have they begun to make significant progress. For example, plant geneticists have found out which gene in roses codes for color, and they have been able to isolate this gene. By deactivating the gene, they can eliminate a particular color from future generations of the plant. Plant color can also be changed by altering the pH of plant cells.

Plant geneticists have also been able to change plant color by switching genes between different plant species. For instance, in roses they have turned off the gene that creates flavonoids, the pigments that produce red and blue colors, and added genes that create carotenoids, the yellow-orange pigments found in corn and carrots, creating new colors of roses. As plant geneticists continue their experiments, an even greater variety of colors will become available for flowers and other plants.

1. Recognizing Words in Context

Find the word *deactivating* in the passage. One definition below is closest to the meaning of that word. One definition has the opposite or nearly opposite meaning. The remaining definition has a completely different meaning. Label the definitions C for *closest*, O for *opposite or nearly opposite*, and D for *different*.

_____ a. turning off

_____ b. turning on

_____ c. turning around

2. Distinguishing Fact from Opinion

Two of the statements below present *facts*, which can be proved correct. The other statement is an *opinion*, which expresses someone's thoughts or beliefs. Label the statements F for *fact* and O for *opinion*.

_____ a. Roses will become more beautiful as they are created in a greater variety of colors.

_____ b. Flavonoids are pigments that produce red and blue colors.

_____ c. Plant geneticists can completely remove the gene that codes for plant color.

3. Keeping Events in Order

Label the statements below 1, 2, and 3 to show the order in which the events happened.

_____ a. Future generations of the rose were a different color.

_____ b. Plant geneticists identified the gene that codes for a particular color in roses.

_____ c. Plant geneticists deactivated the gene that codes for color in roses.

4. Making Correct Inferences

Two of the statements below are correct *inferences,* or reasonable guesses. They are based on information in the passage. The other statement is an incorrect, or faulty, inference. Label the statements C for *correct* inference and F for *faulty* inference.

_____ a. It took plant geneticists a long time to identify color genes because there are many genes.

_____ b. Plants containing the same pigment always have many identical genes.

_____ c. A green pepper and a red apple contain different pigments.

5. Understanding Main Ideas

One of the statements below expresses the main idea of the passage. One statement is too general, or too broad. The other explains only part of the passage; it is too narrow. Label the statements M for *main idea,* B for *too broad,* and N for *too narrow.*

_____ a. Plants have genes that code for color.

_____ b. Plant geneticists are able to identify and manipulate color genes in plants, leading to new color varieties.

_____ c. Carotenoids are yellow-orange pigments found in corn and carrots.

Correct Answers, Part A _____

Correct Answers, Part B _____

Total Correct Answers _____

A biome is an area with a distinctive ecology. In a biome the physical conditions ordinarily remain relatively consistent, and the populations of different life forms remain relatively stable. Some biomes are terrestrial, such as deserts and grasslands, while others are aquatic. Biologists categorize aquatic biomes according to the amount of salt in the water. They have created three categories of aquatic biomes: saltwater, freshwater, and estuary.

Nearly three-fourths of Earth is covered by ocean, and so saltwater biomes form the largest category of aquatic biome. Within these marine communities, the primary factor that distinguishes life forms is the amount of sunlight that penetrates the water. The part of the ocean where sunlight is present is called the photic zone. Phytoplankton, or marine algae, live here. These aquatic plants form the foundation of marine food webs. They rely on sunlight to help them generate their food through photosynthesis. Animals that eat phytoplankton serve as food for larger animals. Without phytoplankton, most marine animals would perish. In addition to providing food, these algae are a major source of oxygen.

Deeper in the ocean is the aphotic zone. Sunlight does not penetrate to this region, so the species found here obtain their energy only by consuming plants and animals. Animals that can move about are called nekton. Animals and plants that attach themselves to the sea floor are called benthos. Some organisms in the aphotic zone serve as decomposers of dead organisms that float down from the photic zone.

Freshwater biomes incorporate such freely moving bodies of water as rivers and streams and such stationary bodies of water as lakes and ponds. The degree of water flow within a freshwater biome is a key factor in determining the features of that biome. For example, rooted plants, different species of algae, and insects and insect larvae thrive in biomes based on standing water. In freshwater biomes with moving water, there are fewer plants and insects.

Some rivers and streams empty into the ocean. The area where freshwater and salt water mix together is called an estuary. In estuaries, water circulates in a way that traps plant nutrients. This gives rise to intense biological activity. Estuaries not only support resident waterfowl, reptiles, and mammals but also serve as breeding grounds for many other species. The salt content in estuaries varies with the tides, and so organisms that live in the water must be highly adaptable.

Reading Time _____

Recalling Facts

1. In biomes, the populations of plants and animals tend to _____ over time.
   - ❏ a. remain stable
   - ❏ b. increase
   - ❏ c. decrease

2. _____ biomes are the most extensive type of aquatic biome.
   - ❏ a. Freshwater
   - ❏ b. Saltwater
   - ❏ c. Estuary

3. Marine algae are called
   - ❏ a. phytoplankton.
   - ❏ b. blue-green algae.
   - ❏ c. zooplankton.

4. Ponds and stream are among the types of
   - ❏ a. saltwater biomes.
   - ❏ b. estuaries.
   - ❏ c. freshwater biomes.

5. _____ biomes are land-based biomes.
   - ❏ a. Terrestrial
   - ❏ b. Estuary
   - ❏ c. Aquatic

Understanding Ideas

6. _____ is *not* an example of a freshwater biome.
   - ❏ a. The Mississippi River
   - ❏ b. Lake Michigan
   - ❏ c. The Caribbean Sea

7. The photic zone is located
   - ❏ a. at the bottom of the ocean.
   - ❏ b. at and near the surface of the ocean.
   - ❏ c. in the middle of warm ocean waters.

8. One can infer that the type of organism most likely to be found in a pool in a deep, dark cave would be a
   - ❏ a. leafy green plant.
   - ❏ b. decomposer.
   - ❏ c. type of algae.

9. One can conclude that at high tide the water in an estuary is
   - ❏ a. saltier than usual.
   - ❏ b. less salty than usual.
   - ❏ c. free of salt.

10. Ecologists involved in the preservation of ocean species likely would be most concerned about
    - ❏ a. fishing boats that bring in hundreds of salmon each day.
    - ❏ b. a group of sharks that eats entire schools of fish.
    - ❏ c. pollution that kills phytoplankton.

The National Wildlife Federation is charged with the protection of natural habitats throughout the United States. Its staff works closely with national and state officials to make sure that people comply with laws regarding wildlife and their ecosystems. Every year the federation inducts important wildlife conservationists into its Conservation Hall of Fame.

Ira Gabrielson (1890–1977) was inducted into the Hall of Fame in 1978. He began his career as a field biologist for the federal government's Bureau of Biological Survey. He helped create laws that provided funding for wildlife conservation. One such law is the Migratory Bird Hunting and Conservation Stamp Act of 1934. Popularly called the Duck Stamp Act, this law requires duck hunters to purchase a large stamp that they sign and keep with them while hunting. Revenue from stamp sales has helped fund the establishment of wildlife conservation programs in many states. Gabrielson also helped obtain passage of the Pittman-Robertson Act, which places a tax on the sale of firearms and ammunition. The revenue from this tax also has been used to fund conservation efforts.

When the Bureau of Biological Service became the U.S. Fish and Wildlife Service in 1940, Gabrielson was appointed its first director. In this post he was responsible for adding huge areas of land to the National Wildlife Refuge System.

1. **Recognizing Words in Context**

   Find the word *inducts* in the passage. One definition below is closest to the meaning of that word. One definition has the opposite or nearly opposite meaning. The remaining definition has a completely different meaning. Label the definitions C for *closest*, O for *opposite or nearly opposite*, and D for *different*.

   _____ a. takes out

   _____ b. lifts up

   _____ c. puts in

2. **Distinguishing Fact from Opinion**

   Two of the statements below present *facts*, which can be proved correct. The other statement is an *opinion*, which expresses someone's thoughts or beliefs. Label the statements F for *fact* and O for *opinion*.

   _____ a. The Pittman-Robertson Act has helped fund conservation efforts.

   _____ b. Everyone needs to be concerned about wildlife preservation.

   _____ c. Ira Gabrielson is in the National Wildlife Federation's Conservation Hall of Fame.

3. **Keeping Events in Order**

Label the statements below 1, 2, and 3 to show the order in which the events happened.

_____ a. Gabrielson began working as a field biologist at the Bureau of Biological Survey.

_____ b. Gabrielson was inducted into the Conservation Hall of Fame.

_____ c. Gabrielson helped pass the Duck Stamp Act and the Pittman-Robertson Act.

4. **Making Correct Inferences**

Two of the statements below are correct *inferences,* or reasonable guesses. They are based on information in the passage. The other statement is an incorrect, or faulty, inference. Label the statements C for *correct* inference and F for *faulty* inference.

_____ a. Thousands of species would be extinct if it were not for the efforts of Ira Gabrielson.

_____ b. Prior to the passage of the Duck Stamp Act, some states did not have wildlife conservation programs.

_____ c. The National Wildlife Refuge System is much larger now than it was in 1940.

5. **Understanding Main Ideas**

One of the statements below expresses the main idea of the passage. One statement is too general, or too broad. The other explains only part of the passage; it is too narrow. Label the statements M for *main idea,* B for *too broad,* and N for *too narrow.*

_____ a. The federal government has established wildlife conservation programs.

_____ b. Ira Gabrielson made many valuable contributions to wildlife conservation.

_____ c. Ira Gabrielson helped obtain passage of the Pittman-Robertson Act.

Correct Answers, Part A _____

Correct Answers, Part B _____

Total Correct Answers _____

Robots and Humans: An Uneasy Partnership

Robots can take many forms. Whether they are toys designed to walk and speak a few phrases or machines programmed to perform complex tasks in factories, robots spark people's imaginations. Regardless of their complexity or function, robots are basically machines designed to perform specific tasks. Often they do work formerly done by humans, but they can only complete the tasks they are programmed to do.

A Czechoslovakian writer named Karel Čapek introduced the term *robot* in his 1920 play *R.U.R.* ("Rossum's Universal Robots"). *Robot* comes from a Czech word meaning "forced labor." Čapek's play centered on the potential dangers of a technologically advanced society, with a group of robots nearly conquering the human race. Although many other people have since warned of the dangers of relying too heavily on technology, robots certainly provide practical benefits.

One way in which robots aid people is by doing repetitive tasks. They are used in a variety of industries and work at little cost beyond that of building and maintaining the machines. For example, in the automotive industry, robots attach parts and move cars along an assembly line. Human workers perform some of the assembly tasks and check the robots' work. In this way, robots and people work side by side.

Unlike humans, robots lack independent thought, so their uses are limited. As advances continue to be made in the field of artificial intelligence, however, the roles of robots will grow to encompass new and more involved tasks. As desirable as this seems, advances in robot technology may also bring renewed concern about the issues first raised by Karel Čapek.

Various popular films and books have sounded a warning of potential danger from the new technology. The fears they prompt have, to some extent, hindered the development of advanced robots and artificial intelligence systems. A science fiction writer named Isaac Asimov wrote several books about robots. In them, he proposed three universal laws that creators of robots ought to follow if their creations are to coexist with humans.

Asimov's first law states that robots must never injure human beings. The second law requires that robots must always obey the commands of human beings. The third law states that although robots have the right to protect their own existence, they must never endanger human beings in doing so. Although laws like these may seem unnecessary today, issues concerning robots and human safety may become more important in the future.

Reading Time _____

Recalling Facts

1. A robot is a
   - ❑ a. machine that thinks independently.
   - ❑ b. machine designed to perform specific tasks.
   - ❑ c. device that operates a computer.

2. Robotic machines are currently used to build
   - ❑ a. cars.
   - ❑ b. computer software.
   - ❑ c. artificial brains.

3. Unlike humans, robots lack
   - ❑ a. reliability.
   - ❑ b. independent thought.
   - ❑ c. precise movement.

4. Robots help people by performing
   - ❑ a. repetitive tasks.
   - ❑ b. only tasks people are incapable of performing.
   - ❑ c. tasks that require creative problem solving.

5. Three universal laws governing robot behavior were proposed by
   - ❑ a. Karel Čapek.
   - ❑ b. Isaac Newton.
   - ❑ c. Isaac Asimov.

Understanding Ideas

6. One can infer that one reason some people have become concerned about robots is that
   - ❑ a. some people have lost their jobs to robots.
   - ❑ b. robots have killed many people.
   - ❑ c. robots are likely to gain control of entire countries.

7. Existing robotic technology is best suited for
   - ❑ a. writing instructional manuals.
   - ❑ b. child care.
   - ❑ c. planetary exploration.

8. From the article, one can infer that robots have replaced some automotive workers because
   - ❑ a. there is a shortage of workers.
   - ❑ b. it costs less to use robots for some assembly work.
   - ❑ c. automotive workers would rather work in other industries.

9. One can conclude that some people oppose the development of intelligent robots because
   - ❑ a. they fear that humans will lose control of robots.
   - ❑ b. robots would become smarter than any human.
   - ❑ c. robot technology has done more harm than good.

10. One can infer that robots are suitable for repetitive tasks because
    - ❑ a. they are extremely precise and they do not get tired.
    - ❑ b. no humans want to do repetitive tasks.
    - ❑ c. labor laws prevent people from doing repetitive tasks.

The future of robotics is bright. Scientists and researchers are finding innovative uses for robots, many of which promise to change the world in a positive way. One promising application of robotic technology is in surgery. By using robot surgeons along with traditional ones, the medical community has improved the effectiveness of some surgical procedures.

Coronary bypass surgery is one type of surgery in which robots are playing an effective role. In bypass surgery, doctors attach a section of vein to a blocked artery so that blood can flow through the vein and around the blockage. Cardiac surgeons have begun using robots to help attach veins and have achieved a rate of success that is higher than that of traditional surgery.

Doctors are also using robots in endoscopic surgery. The goal of this type of surgery is to gain access to the internal parts of the body that require surgery without making long incisions, or cuts. Such incisions take a long time to heal and bring the risk of infection. In endoscopic surgery, the doctor makes only small incisions in the body and inserts a cable containing a tiny camera through one of the incisions. He or she then inserts long surgical tools through other incisions and uses the camera to position and use the tools correctly. Surgeons have begun using robotic devices to help move the surgical tools precisely.

1. **Recognizing Words in Context**

   Find the word *innovative* in the passage. One definition below is closest to the meaning of that word. One definition has the opposite or nearly opposite meaning. The remaining definition has a completely different meaning. Label the definitions C for *closest,* O for *opposite or nearly opposite,* and D for *different.*

   _____ a. new

   _____ b. complex

   _____ c. usual

2. **Distinguishing Fact from Opinion**

   Two of the statements below present *facts,* which can be proved correct. The other statement is an *opinion,* which expresses someone's thoughts or beliefs. Label the statements F for *fact* and O for *opinion.*

   _____ a. Robotic devices are being used in surgery.

   _____ b. Endoscopic surgery does not require long incisions.

   _____ c. The most intelligent surgeons use robots.

3. **Keeping Events in Order**

   Label the statements below 1, 2, and 3 to show the order in which the events happen.

   _____ a. Heart surgeons begin using robots in bypass surgery.

   _____ b. The first coronary bypass surgery is performed.

   _____ c. Surgeons achieve a high rate of success using robots in bypass surgery.

4. **Making Correct Inferences**

   Two of the statements below are correct *inferences,* or reasonable guesses. They are based on information in the passage. The other statement is an incorrect, or faulty, inference. Label the statements C for *correct* inference and F for *faulty* inference.

   _____ a. Robots will eventually replace most doctors in operating rooms.

   _____ b. Patients recover more quickly from endoscopic surgery than they do from traditional surgery.

   _____ c. Robots will be used more and more in medical procedures.

5. **Understanding Main Ideas**

   One of the statements below expresses the main idea of the passage. One statement is too general, or too broad. The other explains only part of the passage; it is too narrow. Label the statements M for *main idea,* B for *too broad,* and N for *too narrow.*

   _____ a. Heart surgeons have used robots to attach veins during bypass surgery.

   _____ b. Doctors are using robots to make surgeries more successful.

   _____ c. Technological advances are continually being made in the medical field.

Correct Answers, Part A _____

Correct Answers, Part B _____

Total Correct Answers _____

Kinds of Dinosaurs

For more than 100 million years, dinosaurs were the dominant animals on Earth. Dinosaur species adapted to their habitats in diverse ways. Although they existed for only a small portion of Earth's history, they ruled the planet longer than any other type of land-dwelling animal. Many scientists think dinosaurs became extinct partly as a result of their generally large size and tremendous energy needs.

Dinosaurs evolved nearly 250 million years ago during a time in history known as the Triassic period of the Mesozoic era. Their sizes ranged from that of a chicken to that of a blue whale. Although they are thought to have evolved from the same ancestors that produced modern reptiles, they differed in important ways from the reptiles that exist today. For example, the dinosaurs' hip structure caused their legs to lie underneath their bodies instead of on the sides of their bodies as seen in such modern reptiles as alligators. This allowed some species to walk upright.

Dinosaurs possessed a wide range of traits. Paleontologists, scientists who study fossils, theorize that there were marked differences not only in the sizes of different dinosaur species but also in their energy needs, skin texture, and speed and manner of movement. One basic difference was that some dinosaurs were carnivorous, whereas others were herbivorous.

One of the largest carnivorous dinosaurs was *Tyrannosaurus rex*. An average tyrannosaurus was about 12 meters (39 feet) long and approximately 5.5 meters (18 feet) tall when standing fully upright. Usually, however, it held its body parallel to the ground, keeping its powerful tail extended behind it for balance. Its mouth contained more than 60 knifelike teeth, some longer than a human hand. Like modern hunting animals, the tyrannosaurus also had forward-facing eyes, allowing good depth perception, and a narrow snout, which gave it unobstructed vision.

In contrast, the triceratops was a herbivore and possessed distinctly different traits. The triceratops was roughly 9 meters (30 feet) long and had a huge head that accounted for almost one-third of its entire body length. At the base of its head was a broad bony structure that resembled a collar. Its teeth were used mostly for grinding and were relatively flat, like those of many modern herbivores. Also, like such modern plant eaters as elk and caribou, the triceratops had hornlike structures protruding from its head. The three horns helped it to defend itself from predators.

Reading Time _____

Recalling Facts

1. Dinosaurs evolved on Earth during the
   - ❑ a. Triassic period.
   - ❑ b. Jurassic period.
   - ❑ c. Cretaceous period.

2. An example of a carnivorous dinosaur is
   - ❑ a. triceratops.
   - ❑ b. tyrannosaurus.
   - ❑ c. iguanadon.

3. Scientists who study dinosaur remains are called
   - ❑ a. geologists.
   - ❑ b. paleontologists.
   - ❑ c. botanists.

4. Some dinosaurs differed from modern reptiles in their ability to walk
   - ❑ a. flat on the ground.
   - ❑ b. upright.
   - ❑ c. rapidly.

5. Dinosaurs ruled Earth for more than
   - ❑ a. 1 billion years.
   - ❑ b. 100 billion years.
   - ❑ c. 100 million years.

Understanding Ideas

6. One can conclude from the article that dinosaurs ranged so widely in size because
   - ❑ a. some were healthier than others.
   - ❑ b. there were many types of dinosaurs.
   - ❑ c. as dinosaurs evolved they became smaller and smaller.

7. One can conclude that dinosaurs survived for so long because
   - ❑ a. Earth did not change when they were alive.
   - ❑ b. they were the most intelligent animals prior to humans.
   - ❑ c. they adjusted well to gradual changes in their environment.

8. Animals with legs on the sides of their bodies are probably best adapted to
   - ❑ a. forest environments.
   - ❑ b. aquatic environments.
   - ❑ c. land-based environments.

9. The most likely cause of the tyrannosaurus's developing long teeth would be the
   - ❑ a. quality of its diet.
   - ❑ b. strength of its jaws.
   - ❑ c. size of its prey.

10. One can conclude that the head of the triceratops is best designed for
    - ❑ a. killing prey.
    - ❑ b. defense.
    - ❑ c. reaching tree branches.

The world of dinosaurs has been brought to life through the efforts of artists such as John Payne. Payne creates movable three-dimensional sculptures of dinosaurs based on fossil records and fossil analysis by scientists. He calls his sculptures Kinetosaurs, a name that he derived from the Greek word *kinetos*, which means "moving," as in "kinetic energy."

By studying the structure of dinosaur bones, biologists are able to determine the range of motion available to various dinosaur species. Payne's sculptures and computer imaging simulations are two ways in which art and science work together to re-create visually the movements of extinct animals.

As scientists have learned more about the way dinosaurs moved, they have disproved some long-held theories about dinosaurs. For example, about 100 years ago scientists concluded that large herbivorous dinosaurs, such as brachiosaurus, must have stretched out their long necks to eat leaves from the upper branches of trees, much as such modern herbivores as giraffes do. However, largely because of the efforts of Payne and others who have simulated dinosaur motion, some scientists now believe it was impossible for these dinosaurs to move in this way. They have calculated that the necks of these dinosaurs were too heavy to lift so high and that the dinosaurs must have grazed on grasses, the way modern zebras do.

1. **Recognizing Words in Context**

   Find the word *derived* in the passage. One definition below is closest to the meaning of that word. One definition has the opposite or nearly opposite meaning. The remaining definition has a completely different meaning. Label the definitions C for *closest*, O for *opposite or nearly opposite,* and D for *different.*

   _____ a. switched around

   _____ b. gave to

   _____ c. took from

2. **Distinguishing Fact from Opinion**

   Two of the statements below present *facts,* which can be proved correct. The other statement is an *opinion,* which expresses someone's thoughts or beliefs. Label the statements F for *fact* and O for *opinion.*

   _____ a. Biologists can use computer imaging to simulate dinosaur motion.

   _____ b. Kinetosaurs are one of the most important developments in the study of dinosaurs.

   _____ c. Kinetosaurs are an artist's portrayal of dinosaurs in motion.

3. Keeping Events in Order

Label the statements below 1, 2, and 3 to show the order in which the events happen.

_____ a. John Payne creates Kinetosaurs.

_____ b. John Payne begins to study the fossil remains of dinosaurs.

_____ c. Scientists use Kinetosaurs in their study of dinosaurs.

4. Making Correct Inferences

Two of the statements below are correct *inferences,* or reasonable guesses. They are based on information in the passage. The other statement is an incorrect, or faulty, inference. Label the statements C for *correct* inference and F for *faulty* inference.

_____ a. Kinetosaurs show the types of motion dinosaurs were capable of.

_____ b. The accurateness of Kinetosaurs is limited by current knowledge of dinosaurs.

_____ c. Kinetosaurs are the most accurate models of dinosaurs in motion.

5. Understanding Main Ideas

One of the statements below expresses the main idea of the passage. One statement is too general, or too broad. The other explains only part of the passage; it is too narrow. Label the statements M for *main idea,* B for *too broad,* and N for *too narrow.*

_____ a. Realistic models of dinosaurs have been created.

_____ b. The word *Kinetosaur* comes from the root word *kinetos* meaning "moving."

_____ c. John Payne mixes art and science to create realistic models of dinosaurs in motion.

Correct Answers, Part A _____

Correct Answers, Part B _____

Total Correct Answers _____

Chemistry in Everyday Life

Chemistry is a discipline that deals with some of the most fundamental aspects of the universe. Everything we see and touch is made up of the smallest units of matter, called atoms. There are at least 114 types of atoms. These types are called elements. Most of the things on Earth consist of combinations of only the 20 most common elements.

To appreciate how atoms form substances, one should first understand the basic structure of atoms. Atoms consist of protons, neutrons, and electrons. Protons and neutrons form the nucleus of an atom, and electrons lie outside the nucleus. Elements differ in the number of protons in each atom. When the atoms of different elements combine by forming electrostatic bonds, they share or transfer electrons. Electrostatic bonds in which one atom transfers an electron to another atom are weaker than those in which an electron is shared. The way in which atoms bond determines the type of substances they form. For example, a water molecule is formed when one oxygen atom shares electrons with two hydrogen atoms; a molecule of table salt is formed when a sodium atom transfers an electron to a chlorine atom.

Choosing construction materials illustrates one practical application of chemistry. Manufacturers combine various elements to create substances for specific types of construction. For example, if engineers want to build a bridge with cables, they generally will use cables made from steel. Steel is made from the elements iron and carbon, and it can withstand great tensile stress, or pulling. In contrast, when engineers need a material that can withstand a compressive type of stress, they often use bricks made of clay that contains the elements aluminum and silicon.

Chemistry also plays an important role in the creation of ordinary household products. Halogens are chemically similar elements used in many common products. Halogens are a very reactive group of elements because they require only one other electron to become completely stable. Because of this, they tend to react very quickly and bond tightly. An example of one such halogen is fluorine. Fluoride, a compound of fluorine, is used in toothpaste because it bonds to tooth enamel and helps replace enamel lost through tooth decay. Chlorine is another example of a halogen. Like fluorine, chlorine is very reactive; it is commonly used to whiten laundry because chlorine molecules bond tightly to dirt particles, allowing water to separate them from fabric.

Reading Time _____

Recalling Facts

1. Atoms bond by sharing or transferring
   - ❑ a. protons.
   - ❑ b. electrons.
   - ❑ c. neutrons.

2. A molecule of table salt is formed when a chlorine atom _____ a sodium atom.
   - ❑ a. receives an electron from
   - ❑ b. shares an electron with
   - ❑ c. eliminates an electron from

3. A group of chemically similar elements that are just one electron short of being stable consists of the
   - ❑ a. noble gases.
   - ❑ b. halogens.
   - ❑ c. metals.

4. An element used to whiten laundry is
   - ❑ a. chlorine.
   - ❑ b. fluorine.
   - ❑ c. sodium.

5. Most substances on Earth are combinations of some of the _____ most common elements.
   - ❑ a. 62
   - ❑ b. 40
   - ❑ c. 20

Understanding Ideas

6. One can infer that the nucleus lies at the _____ of an atom.
   - ❑ a. edge
   - ❑ b. corner
   - ❑ c. center

7. It can be inferred from the article that different mixtures of elements produce materials with
   - ❑ a. different strengths.
   - ❑ b. identical strengths.
   - ❑ c. closely related characteristics.

8. Which of the following statements is most likely true?
   - ❑ a. All detergents use halogens.
   - ❑ b. Certain elements have a tendency to transfer electrons and others to share electrons.
   - ❑ c. Only halogens bond tightly to other elements.

9. It can be inferred from the article that elements requiring more than one electron to be stable are
   - ❑ a. more reactive than halogens.
   - ❑ b. not reactive at all.
   - ❑ c. less reactive than halogens.

10. One can infer from the article that some elements
    - ❑ a. have identical properties.
    - ❑ b. are rarely seen.
    - ❑ c. have no protons.

Organic farming is becoming more common. This type of farming is now being used in more than 160 countries and continues to grow in popularity. Some cultures have always used organic farming, whereas others are returning to it. Leading the push for organic farming in countries that once abandoned it are people who think that many agricultural chemicals are unnecessary and even detrimental. More and more people are choosing to consume organically grown food.

Organic farming differs from most modern farming methods because it does not involve the use of chemical pesticides and chemical fertilizers. Many farmers who use modern methods specialize in one crop. They must use pesticides because growing the same crop every year provides fertile breeding grounds for insects that feed on that particular crop. In contrast, organic farmers rely on old-fashioned methods to control insect populations. They plant different kinds of crops and change their locations from year to year to prevent insects from congregating in a particular area.

Organic farming is not limited to those farmers who grow produce. Farmers who raise livestock also can use organic methods. Organic farmers raise livestock without using such additives as growth hormones and antibiotics. Using antibiotics unnecessarily can result in the development of highly resistant strains of bacteria.

1. **Recognizing Words in Context**

Find the word *detrimental* in the passage. One definition below is closest to the meaning of that word. One definition has the opposite or nearly opposite meaning. The remaining definition has a completely different meaning. Label the definitions C for *closest*, O for *opposite or nearly opposite*, and D for *different*.

_____ a. meaningful

_____ b. helpful

_____ c. harmful

2. **Distinguishing Fact from Opinion**

Two of the statements below present *facts*, which can be proved correct. The other statement is an *opinion*, which expresses someone's thoughts or beliefs. Label the statements F for *fact* and O for *opinion*.

_____ a. Organic farmers do not use chemical pesticides to control insect populations.

_____ b. The growth of organic farming is a positive development.

_____ c. Organic livestock farmers do not use hormones and antibiotics.

3. Keeping Events in Order

Label the statements below 1, 2, and 3 to show the order in which the events happen.

_____ a. Organic crops are harvested for the first time in many years.

_____ b. Farmers in a state begin to grow crops without the use of artificial chemicals.

_____ c. Organic produce becomes available at supermarkets.

4. Making Correct Inferences

Two of the statements below are correct *inferences,* or reasonable guesses. They are based on information in the passage. The other statement is an incorrect, or faulty, inference. Label the statements C for *correct* inference and F for *faulty* inference.

_____ a. Organic farming is not the most popular method of farming among farmers in the United States.

_____ b. All pesticides are harmful to humans.

_____ c. Most organic farmers do not lose high percentages of their crops to insects.

5. Understanding Main Ideas

One of the statements below expresses the main idea of the passage. One statement is too general, or too broad. The other explains only part of the passage; it is too narrow. Label the statements M for *main idea,* B for *too broad,* and N for *too narrow.*

_____ a. Farming methods vary from region to region.

_____ b. Organic farming, the production of food without the use of chemicals, is gaining in popularity.

_____ c. Organic farmers do not use chemical fertilizers.

Correct Answers, Part A _____

Correct Answers, Part B _____

Total Correct Answers _____

The Mayan civilization of Central America and southern Mexico was an advanced culture. This civilization reached its peak from about A.D. 250 to 900. One of the greatest achievements of the Maya was developing a sophisticated system of astronomy that employed precise methods for predicting the movements of the Sun, Moon, and other heavenly bodies.

One of the astronomical goals of the Maya was to calculate the position of the Sun at various latitudes throughout the day and year. Each day they carefully charted the position of the Sun in relation to the horizon and the zenith. The zenith is the point in the sky directly above the observer. When the Sun is at its zenith, it casts no shadow, and this fascinated the Maya. They kept track of the number of days between the time the Sun was at its zenith and the solstices. Solstices occur at the beginning of winter and the beginning of summer. Equinoxes occur at the beginning of spring and the beginning of autumn. The Maya constructed a pyramid in such a way that on the equinoxes, a snake-shaped shadow moved along a staircase. In these ways, the Maya were able to determine the change of seasons.

The Maya were especially interested in Venus. Through their detailed observations, they determined the cyclic motion of Venus and the number of days it took Venus to reach various positions in relation to the Sun. Among their findings was that as Venus moved through the night sky over a period of months, it seemed to disappear, stop, and change directions. Despite their lack of scientific instruments, they made some sound conclusions. For example, they understood that when Venus could not be seen from Earth, it was because Venus was passing between Earth and the Sun. The Maya timed many of their military attacks to coincide with the time that Venus appeared stationary. They performed prayer rituals to ward off natural disasters during the eight days when Venus disappeared from their view. Mayan kings were crowned only when Earth and Venus were aligned with the Sun.

The Maya also paid careful attention to the lunar cycle. Like modern-day astronomers, they knew there are 29.5 days between full moons. This was reflected in their calendars, which alternated between 29 days and 30 days per month, much like ours. Mayan calendars are considered to be more accurate than those of any other ancient civilization.

Reading Time _____

Recalling Facts

1. The Mayan civilization was in
   - ❏ a. Mexico and Central America.
   - ❏ b. West Africa.
   - ❏ c. South America.

2. The Maya were particularly interested in
   - ❏ a. Venus.
   - ❏ b. Mars.
   - ❏ c. Saturn.

3. The equinoxes mark the
   - ❏ a. beginning of winter and the beginning of summer.
   - ❏ b. beginning of spring and the beginning of autumn.
   - ❏ c. time when the Sun is at its zenith in Central America.

4. Mayan kings were crowned when
   - ❏ a. Venus appeared stationary in the night sky.
   - ❏ b. Venus disappeared from view.
   - ❏ c. Earth and Venus were aligned with the Sun.

5. Mayan months had
   - ❏ a. 28 or 31 days.
   - ❏ b. 30 or 31 days.
   - ❏ c. 29 or 30 days.

Understanding Ideas

6. One can conclude from the article that Mayan astronomy was
   - ❏ a. simplistic in its approach.
   - ❏ b. sophisticated and precise despite the lack of technologically advanced instruments.
   - ❏ c. imprecise and dominated by superstition.

7. One can conclude that Mayan astronomers were notable for their
   - ❏ a. careful observation and record keeping.
   - ❏ b. use of telescopes and sundials.
   - ❏ c. charts of constellations.

8. One can infer that being aware of the changing seasons was important for the Maya because
   - ❏ a. they did little work between the autumn equinox and the spring equinox.
   - ❏ b. winter was a time of continual religious pageants.
   - ❏ c. they were an agricultural people.

9. One can conclude that the Maya thought that the time when the planets were aligned was a time of
   - ❏ a. potential danger.
   - ❏ b. great significance.
   - ❏ c. uncertainty about the future.

10. One can infer that the accuracy of the Mayan calendar was due to
    - ❏ a. Mayan libraries of books from ancient Greece.
    - ❏ b. information brought by Roman armies.
    - ❏ c. Mayan studies of the Sun and Moon.

Calendars Across the Ages

Calendars are the tools that cultures use to record the passage of time. Throughout history, there have been almost as many calendars as there have been civilizations. The modern calendar, usually called the Gregorian calendar, was developed at the request of Pope Gregory XIII in the 16th century. It is organized into days, weeks, months, and years.

The Gregorian calendar has characteristics similar to many earlier calendars. For example, the concept of a leap year, or a day added every fourth year, originally came from the Julian calendar introduced by Julius Caesar in 46 B.C. Likewise, our calendar is in some ways commensurate with the ancient Islamic calendar, which also is based on a 12-month year.

One difference between the Gregorian and Islamic calendars is the length of the year. The Gregorian calendar is based on Earth's 365.25-day period of revolution, or the time Earth takes to orbit the Sun. Therefore, the average length of the Gregorian month is 30.44 days (12 months × 30.44 days = 365.25). In contrast the Islamic calendar is based on the period of the Moon's rotation around Earth, which is 29.5 days. As a result, each of its 12 months has a length of 29.5 days, and the Islamic year is usually only 354 days. Some Islamic years have an extra day to make up for small differences in the length of the lunar year.

1. **Recognizing Words in Context**

   Find the word *commensurate* in the passage. One definition below is closest to the meaning of that word. One definition has the opposite or nearly opposite meaning. The remaining definition has a completely different meaning. Label the definitions C for *closest*, O for *opposite or nearly opposite*, and D for *different*.

   _____ a. measured in the same way

   _____ b. measured differently

   _____ c. originating from the same source

2. **Distinguishing Fact from Opinion**

   Two of the statements below present *facts*, which can be proved correct. The other statement is an *opinion*, which expresses someone's thoughts or beliefs. Label the statements F for *fact* and O for *opinion*.

   _____ a. The Julian calendar was introduced in 46 B.C.

   _____ b. The period of Earth's revolution is 365.25 days.

   _____ c. The Julian calendar is not very useful.

3. Keeping Events in Order

Label the statements below 1, 2, and 3 to show the order in which the events happened.

_____ a. Julius Caesar introduced the Julian calendar.

_____ b. The United States of America adopted the Gregorian calendar.

_____ c. The Gregorian calendar was introduced.

4. Making Correct Inferences

Two of the statements below are correct *inferences*, or reasonable guesses. They are based on information in the passage. The other statement is an incorrect, or faulty, inference. Label the statements C for *correct* inference and F for *faulty* inference.

_____ a. The Gregorian calendar measures Earth's revolution more precisely than the Julian calendar did.

_____ b. Ancient calendars were highly inaccurate.

_____ c. Some calendars are based on astronomical data.

5. Understanding Main Ideas

One of the statements below expresses the main idea of the passage. One statement is too general, or too broad. The other explains only part of the passage; it is too narrow. Label the statements M for *main idea*, B for *too broad*, and N for *too narrow*.

_____ a. Many different calendars have been developed throughout history.

_____ b. Different civilizations have measured time differently.

_____ c. The Gregorian calendar is based on Earth's period of revolution around the Sun.

Correct Answers, Part A _____

Correct Answers, Part B _____

Total Correct Answers _____

The Early Development of Meteorology

It is hard to pinpoint the exact origin of meteorology. Although it seems likely that prehistoric peoples must have attempted to predict weather conditions because it would have helped them in growing crops, they left no written accounts of whatever methods they used.

The first comprehensive written account of weather occurred in the time of the famous Greek scientist and philosopher Aristotle. The term *meteorology* comes from *Meteorologica,* a book of observations attributed to Aristotle. The book, which appeared in about 380 B.C., deals with topics that include clouds, rain, wind, lightning, and thunder. Although many of the theories in the book proved to be wrong, it generated interest in the subject of meteorology.

It was not until the 16th and 17th centuries that meteorology began to develop as a true science. During this time, scientists became aware that changes in certain conditions of air were related to changes in weather. To better predict these changes, they devised simple instruments to measure such conditions as temperature, pressure, and humidity.

One of the first important inventions in meteorology was a thermometer developed by the brilliant Italian scientist Galileo Galilei in 1593. This thermometer worked on the principle that as the temperature of water changes, so does its density. Although Galileo's thermometer was not very precise, it created great interest throughout Europe. People sought to develop tools that were more accurate, and the science of meteorology began to flourish.

Evangelista Torricelli, an assistant to Galileo and a talented scientist in his own right, invented the first barometer in 1643. This device consisted of a glass tube filled with liquid mercury. The level of the mercury varied with the pressure of the surrounding air. Scientists began to understand the importance of air pressure in meteorology as they observed a relationship between air pressure and wind.

In the early 1700s, Daniel Fahrenheit of Germany made an accurate mercury thermometer, creating his own scale to measure temperature. In this scale he classified the freezing point of water at 32 degrees and the boiling point of water at 212 degrees. In this way he standardized temperature. It could now be compared against his standard scale.

Another important invention was the hygrometer developed by Horace de Saussure of Switzerland in 1783. This tool measured humidity. Using the measurements of all these devices, scientists were better able to make predictions about the weather.

Reading Time _____

Recalling Facts

1. The first important work on meteorology consisted of a set of observations attributed to
   - ❏ a. Galileo.
   - ❏ b. Aristotle.
   - ❏ c. Leonardo da Vinci.

2. The first important devices for measuring the physical conditions of air appeared in the
   - ❏ a. 16th and 17th centuries.
   - ❏ b. 5th and 6th centuries.
   - ❏ c. 19th and 20th centuries.

3. Galileo invented an early type of
   - ❏ a. barometer.
   - ❏ b. hygrometer.
   - ❏ c. thermometer.

4. A barometer measures
   - ❏ a. temperature.
   - ❏ b. humidity.
   - ❏ c. air pressure.

5. A standardized temperature scale was introduced in the early 18th century by
   - ❏ a. Descartes.
   - ❏ b. Fahrenheit.
   - ❏ c. Galileo.

Understanding Ideas

6. One can conclude from the article that as technology improved,
   - ❏ a. the accuracy of weather forecasts remained the same.
   - ❏ b. weather forecasting became more accurate.
   - ❏ c. predicting the weather became more important to people.

7. One can infer from the article that weather forecasts
   - ❏ a. depend almost entirely on readings from barometers.
   - ❏ b. are most accurate in regions with extreme climates.
   - ❏ c. are based on a variety of measurements.

8. One can infer that the development of some meteorological instruments was related to the
   - ❏ a. writings of Aristotle.
   - ❏ b. invention of the steam engine.
   - ❏ c. discovery of the properties of mercury.

9. One can conclude from the article that a sudden change in wind speed is most closely related to a change in
   - ❏ a. levels of precipitation.
   - ❏ b. humidity.
   - ❏ c. air pressure.

10. A main idea of the article is that
    - ❏ a. improvements in technology led to improvements in weather forecasting.
    - ❏ b. major advances in meteorology occurred in the 1900s.
    - ❏ c. Galileo contributed to the advancement of science in many ways.

18 B   Weather Proverbs

Weather proverbs have long been an important part of people's relationship with their environment. In the days when literacy was not widespread, farmers and sailors used weather proverbs to help them remember important characteristics of the weather. Weather proverbs employ simple phrases to describe certain tendencies in weather patterns. These proverbs frequently take the form of rhymes, which people find easy to remember.

For example, farmers needed to prepare for thunderstorms by moving their animals inside a barn or other shelter. To ready themselves for possible storms, they used to check the amount of dew on the grass in the mornings, remembering the proverb "When grass is dry in morning light, look for rain before the night."

Similarly, sailors had to be especially well prepared for bad weather because storms could be deadly. To avoid being lost at sea, they had to learn methods for predicting heavy wind and rain; from this need emanated proverbs such as "When seagulls fly to land, a storm is at hand." Sailors also learned to listen to the intensity of the sounds that surrounded the ship, such as the sounds of waves or birds. The way sound resonates can indicate the thickness of air and relative moisture content, as in the proverb "Sound traveling far and wide, a stormy day betide."

1. **Recognizing Words in Context**

   Find the word *emanated* in the passage. One definition below is closest to the meaning of that word. One definition has the opposite or nearly opposite meaning. The remaining definition has a completely different meaning. Label the definitions C for *closest,* O for *opposite or nearly opposite,* and D for *different.*

   _____ a. receded

   _____ b. emerged

   _____ c. maintained

2. **Distinguishing Fact from Opinion**

   Two of the statements below present *facts,* which can be proved correct. The other statement is an *opinion,* which expresses someone's thoughts or beliefs. Label the statements F for *fact* and O for *opinion.*

   _____ a. Weather proverbs are reliable and easy to remember.

   _____ b. Weather proverbs influence some people's expectations about the weather.

   _____ c. Farmers and sailors are two groups of people who have relied on weather proverbs.

3. Keeping Events in Order

Label the statements below 1, 2, and 3 to show the order in which the events happen.

_____ a. A weather proverb turns out to be correct more often than not.

_____ b. A weather proverb gains popularity and is passed down over many generations.

_____ c. People observe weather patterns and create a weather proverb.

4. Making Correct Inferences

Two of the statements below are correct *inferences,* or reasonable guesses. They are based on information in the passage. The other statement is an incorrect, or faulty, inference. Label the statements C for *correct* inference and F for *faulty* inference.

_____ a. Only farmers and sailors use weather proverbs.

_____ b. Weather proverbs sometimes result in incorrect predictions.

_____ c. Proverbs are not the best source of weather information.

5. Understanding Main Ideas

One of the statements below expresses the main idea of the passage. One statement is too general, or too broad. The other explains only part of the passage; it is too narrow. Label the statements M for *main idea,* B for *too broad,* and N for *too narrow.*

_____ a. Some people use weather proverbs to help predict the weather.

_____ b. Some proverbs describe the natural world.

_____ c. One weather proverb concerns morning dew.

Correct Answers, Part A _____

Correct Answers, Part B _____

Total Correct Answers _____

The Biochemist

Biochemistry—the branch of chemistry that deals with living things—is one of science's most complex and least understood disciplines. Biochemists study the biological processes that create and sustain plants and animals. Among the issues they study are some of the greatest mysteries involving life itself, such as how a microscopic egg can turn into a large and complex organism.

Biochemists often specialize in one type of species or process. For example, some biochemists study green plants. Within this realm, there are scientists who focus on photosynthesis. Biochemists who study this process might examine how plants convert the sun's energy into simple sugars or find the way in which these simple sugars are stored in more complex forms, such as starch. Other plant biochemists might be interested in the way certain plant genes are turned on and off, causing the plant to develop in specialized ways. By understanding plant genetics, biochemists may be able to help farmers to increase crop yields or eliminate the need for artificial pesticides.

Another area of interest to many biochemists is human metabolism. Metabolism refers to the chemical changes in cells that involve integrating new material and generating energy for all of an organism's activities. There are two basic metabolic processes. In one, energy is used to build simple molecules into complex molecules. In the other, complex molecules are broken down into simple molecules, releasing energy. For example, ingested food travels down many different biochemical pathways within the body and is slowly changed into energy.

All the metabolic pathways that biochemists study start with the conversion of glucose from food into energy that the body needs to sustain vital functions. These functions, which include movement, tissue repair, and reproduction, each require the body to convert some type of energy into a more usable form. Glucose enters each of the body's billions of cells through its outer cell membrane and is broken down and reassembled into energy storage units, such as adenosine triphosphate, or ATP. This very simple and effective way of storing and releasing energy in cells throughout the body allows for a quick response when energy needs in a specific part of the body are high. For instance, when a person is running a marathon, she or he needs a large amount of energy to power the muscles in the legs but less energy in other parts of the body.

Reading Time _____

Recalling Facts

1. Biochemistry is the chemistry of
   ❏ a. inorganic molecules.
   ❏ b. physical forces.
   ❏ c. living things.

2. One of the topics that biochemists are most interested in is
   ❏ a. behavior.
   ❏ b. metabolism.
   ❏ c. inertia.

3. The way in which a plant develops is determined mainly by
   ❏ a. simple sugars.
   ❏ b. soil type.
   ❏ c. genes.

4. ATP is a type of
   ❏ a. glucose.
   ❏ b. energy-storing compound.
   ❏ c. metabolic process.

5. Energy is _____ when a cell turns simple molecules into complex molecules.
   ❏ a. used
   ❏ b. produced
   ❏ c. conserved

Understanding Ideas

6. One can conclude from the article that animals
   ❏ a. do not obtain energy from substances found in plants.
   ❏ b. have some biological functions that are similar to those of plants.
   ❏ c. have metabolisms and plants do not.

7. It can be inferred that biochemists must understand the basic principles of both
   ❏ a. chemistry and biology.
   ❏ b. botany and paleontology.
   ❏ c. natural science and social science.

8. One can infer that during digestion
   ❏ a. simple molecules are converted to complex molecules.
   ❏ b. simple molecules are rearranged into other simple molecules.
   ❏ c. complex molecules are converted to simple molecules.

9. One can conclude from the article that ATP is present
   ❏ a. within cell membranes only.
   ❏ b. within cells.
   ❏ c. only within vital organs.

10. One can infer that a cell controls which substances enter and leave it through its
    ❏ a. genetic material.
    ❏ b. cell membrane.
    ❏ c. ATP.

The Growing Role of Genetics in Biochemistry

Most modern biochemists find the body's many complex processes a fruitful area of inquiry. One of the discipline's key questions is how the body is able to use food and drink to produce the energy and substances needed for everyday functions. Biochemists have realized that there is no one easy answer to this question. They must be content with understanding complex metabolic agents and processes piece by piece, one step at a time.

Much of the mystery and future direction of biochemistry involves scrutinizing and perhaps adjusting human metabolism. Scientists have found that certain human genes control whether a person becomes obese. They have also found, however, that not everyone with these genes is obese or even overweight. Therefore, something must act in concert with these genes to "turn them on" like a light switch, in effect slowing the human metabolism to a crawl. A slow metabolism results in a high proportion of food being converted into fat.

Unlike their traditional counterparts who merely set out to understand metabolism from a chemical point of view, modern biochemists work with other scientists, such as geneticists, to try to resolve what controls the mechanisms of metabolism. This knowledge may one day improve the quality of people's lives by allowing scientists to speed up slow metabolisms.

1. **Recognizing Words in Context**

   Find the word *scrutinizing* in the passage. One definition below is closest to the meaning of that word. One definition has the opposite or nearly opposite meaning. The remaining definition has a completely different meaning. Label the definitions C for *closest*, O for *opposite or nearly opposite,* and D for *different.*

   _____ a. analyzing

   _____ b. transferring

   _____ c. ignoring

2. **Distinguishing Fact from Opinion**

   Two of the statements below present *facts,* which can be proved correct. The other statement is an *opinion,* which expresses someone's thoughts or beliefs. Label the statements F for *fact* and O for *opinion.*

   _____ a. Biochemical research is of critical importance.

   _____ b. Many biochemists are interested in the study of metabolism.

   _____ c. Some genes appear to be "switched on," while others do not.

3. **Keeping Events in Order**

Label the statements below 1, 2, and 3 to show the order in which the events happen.

_____ a. An obese man starts to lose significant amounts of weight.

_____ b. Biochemists find a way to turn off an obesity gene.

_____ c. A man becomes more and more obese.

4. **Making Correct Inferences**

Two of the statements below are correct *inferences,* or reasonable guesses. They are based on information in the passage. The other statement is an incorrect, or faulty, inference. Label the statements C for *correct* inference and F for *faulty* inference.

_____ a. Increasingly sophisticated technology will enhance biochemical research.

_____ b. The primary goal of biochemistry is to make people healthier.

_____ c. Biochemists work with other scientists besides geneticists.

5. **Understanding Main Ideas**

One of the statements below expresses the main idea of the passage. One statement is too general, or too broad. The other explains only part of the passage; it is too narrow. Label the statements M for *main idea*, B for *too broad,* and N for *too narrow.*

_____ a. Biochemistry is the branch of chemistry that deals with biological processes.

_____ b. Biochemists work with geneticists to study the mechanisms involved in obesity.

_____ c. Biochemists' studies of metabolism are influenced by developments in genetics.

Correct Answers, Part A _____

Correct Answers, Part B _____

Total Correct Answers _____

20 | A | The Science of Bike Riding

Bicycle riding is popular in most parts of the world. In fact, people in some countries rely on bicycles as their primary mode of transportation. Bicycles are actually quite efficient when compared with other vehicles. The same amount of energy that will power a bicycle for 5 kilometers (3.1 miles) will power a car for a mere 88 meters (289 feet). Instead of powering an automobile with gasoline, people can power bicycles with their own bodies and reduce pollution.

Food supplies the fuel that powers the human body. In the case of a bicyclist, the type of food ingested can influence performance. Fruit and other foods that are rich in simple carbohydrates are an effective source for quick energy immediately before a ride. If a cyclist is interested in long-distance performance, however, whole-grain bread and other foods rich in complex carbohydrates are better energy sources and should be eaten an hour or so before riding.

A cyclist also needs protein to help build strong muscles. Calf and thigh muscles provide the strength needed for cycling. These muscle also support the thighbone and shinbone. When a person is riding a bike, the thighbone works like a simple machine called a lever and acts on the shinbone to exert force on the pedals.

Even when cyclists are generating sufficient amounts of energy to power their bikes, air resistance limits their performance. When an object moves through air, it creates wind that pulls the object in the opposite direction. Bicycles that are designed to have the rider sit up straight do nothing to reduce air resistance. Racing bikes, on the other hand, are specifically designed to minimize it.

Designers have done several things to make racing bikes aerodynamic. Some designers have created frames made of tubes with oval or tear-shaped cross-sections instead of traditional round tubes. Others have focused on changing wheel design, using disc wheels instead of the standard spoked wheel. Although the disc wheels are heavier, they create less drag. Spoked wheels act like eggbeaters and cause eddies—or pockets of turbulent air—to travel through the wheel, increasing wind resistance.

Although bicycle designers have succeeded in improving performance with their sleeker designs, the human body will always cause some wind drag. Most racers reduce friction by wearing skintight clothes and specially shaped helmets. Doing this eliminates resistance from loose clothing so that the only drag is over the rider's streamlined body.

Reading Time _____

Recalling Facts

1. Compared with a car, a bicycle is _____ mode of transportation.
   - ❏ a. a less efficient
   - ❏ b. a more efficient
   - ❏ c. an equally efficient

2. To build strong muscles, a cyclist requires adequate amounts of
   - ❏ a. complex carbohydrates.
   - ❏ b. simple carbohydrates.
   - ❏ c. protein.

3. In the human leg, the thighbone acts like a
   - ❏ a. pulley.
   - ❏ b. wedge.
   - ❏ c. lever.

4. Air resistance is sometimes called
   - ❏ a. turbulence.
   - ❏ b. drag.
   - ❏ c. tailwind.

5. If a racer is interested in long-distance performance, a good choice of food would be
   - ❏ a. a chocolate bar.
   - ❏ b. an apple.
   - ❏ c. whole-grain bread.

Understanding Ideas

6. One can conclude from the article that
   - ❏ a. recreational-bike designers and racing-bike designers have some different objectives.
   - ❏ b. racing bikes are painful to ride.
   - ❏ c. the more muscular people are, the more aerodynamic they are.

7. A good way for a bike racer to increase speed would be to
   - ❏ a. buy a bike that has spoked wheels.
   - ❏ b. strengthen the thigh muscles.
   - ❏ c. eat only foods rich in simple carbohydrates.

8. One can assume that bicycles will change as
   - ❏ a. wind conditions change.
   - ❏ b. the needs of riders change.
   - ❏ c. cyclists lengthen the duration of their rides.

9. One can conclude from the article that
   - ❏ a. cyclists need protein in their diets more than any other type of food.
   - ❏ b. different foods provide different energy benefits.
   - ❏ c. the more a cyclist eats, the better his or her long-distance performance.

10. One can infer that another way that racing bikes can be made more efficient is by
   - ❏ a. using lightweight materials.
   - ❏ b. adding tube-shaped spokes.
   - ❏ c. using tires that grip the road better.

Wheels and Roads

The oldest-known wheel was used nearly 6,000 years ago. In ancient times, devices with wheels included carts that carried goods, chariots that transported people, and frames for containers that moved water. Although many inventions have contributed to human progress, few have contributed as much as the wheel.

The widespread use of wheels as a means of transport dates from the Roman era. The Romans realized that wheel efficiency was closely related to how freely a wheel could move. To minimize friction and make wheeled vehicles more practical throughout their region, they developed a large network of paved roads. The Romans are credited as being the first culture to develop roads to facilitate the motion of wheels, but others followed.

During the Industrial Revolution, Europe and the United States each built sophisticated systems of roads. One reason these were needed was that more people and goods were moving into cities. Bicyclists, who grew rapidly in number beginning in the 1880s, availed themselves of the opportunity to use the new roads for smoother rides. It was not until the early 1900s that cars began to dominate the roads, forcing bicyclists out of the center of the road and off to the side.

1. **Recognizing Words in Context**
   Find the word *facilitate* in the passage. One definition below is closest to the meaning of that word. One definition has the opposite or nearly opposite meaning. The remaining definition has a completely different meaning. Label the definitions C for *closest*, O for *opposite or nearly opposite*, and D for *different*.

   _____ a. make easier

   _____ b. organize

   _____ c. interfere with

2. **Distinguishing Fact from Opinion**
   Two of the statements below present *facts*, which can be proved correct. The other statement is an *opinion*, which expresses someone's thoughts or beliefs. Label the statements F for *fact* and O for *opinion*.

   _____ a. Romans needed wheels for their chariots.

   _____ b. The wheel is the single most important invention in history.

   _____ c. The Industrial Revolution led to the creation of a new system of roads.

3. Keeping Events in Order

Label the statements below 1, 2, and 3 to show the order in which the events happened.

_____ a. The wheel was invented.

_____ b. The wheel was first used in transportation devices.

_____ c. The first system of paved roads was developed.

4. Making Correct Inferences

Two of the statements below are correct *inferences,* or reasonable guesses. They are based on information in the passage. The other statement is an incorrect, or faulty, inference. Label the statements C for *correct* inference and F for *faulty* inference.

_____ a. Romans used horses to pull their chariots.

_____ b. Transportation is impossible without wheels.

_____ c. Wheels have been used in many important machines other than vehicles.

5. Understanding Main Ideas

One of the statements below expresses the main idea of the passage. One statement is too general, or too broad. The other explains only part of the passage; it is too narrow. Label the statements M for *main idea,* B for *too broad,* and N for *too narrow.*

_____ a. Some simple devices have had a profound impact on society.

_____ b. The history of the wheel goes back thousands of years.

_____ c. The construction of paved roads has contributed to the evolution of the wheel.

Correct Answers, Part A _____

Correct Answers, Part B _____

Total Correct Answers _____

Smell and Taste

Human beings possess five senses—smell, taste, sight, hearing, and touch. The senses are indispensable because they allow people to function in their environment. This can be seen through a closer examination of the senses of smell and taste.

All the organs involved in the sense of smell combine to make up what is referred to as the olfactory system. The main processes in the olfactory system takes place in the upper portion of the nose. At the top of each nostril are approximately 50 million olfactory receptor cells. Every cell contains a number of tiny hairlike structures called cilia that catch particles and gaseous molecules. These particles cause chemical reactions that in turn create nerve impulses. The impulses travel to the brain, which interprets them as various smells. The olfactory cells are highly sensitive and can detect extremely low concentrations of molecules in the air. For example, a person can smell smoke from a great distance if the wind is blowing in the right direction.

People's sense of smell often elicits strong emotional response. Many scientists believe that this is because the sense of smell is connected directly to the limbic system of the brain, the section that is associated with emotions. Virtually no other sense can trigger such intense emotions and vivid memories as the sense of smell. Studies have demonstrated that one of the aromas most preferred by both men and women is the aroma of freshly baked bread, perhaps because it elicits sentimental memories of childhood.

This connection between smell and emotion helps drive the fragrance industry. Research has shown that a person can be perceived as more attractive when wearing a particular fragrance. Yet fragrances affect different people in different ways. Perfume or cologne that may smell good to one person may produce negative feelings in another.

Smell is approximately 10,000 times stronger than taste, but the two senses are closely interrelated. Although humans have thousands of taste buds, each with approximately 50 receptors, they can distinguish just four fundamental tastes. These are sweet, sour, bitter, and salty; every unique flavor is simply a combination of these four tastes as they are experienced together with the sense of smell.

The important role that smell plays in the perception of taste becomes apparent to a person who has a cold or other respiratory infection. When nasal passages are congested, foods lack much of their usual flavor.

Reading Time _____

Recalling Facts

1. All the organs involved in our sense of smell make up what is called the
   - ❑ a. olfactory system.
   - ❑ b. limbic system.
   - ❑ c. proboscis system.

2. Our sense of smell is closely connected with our sense of
   - ❑ a. sight.
   - ❑ b. taste.
   - ❑ c. touch.

3. Humans can distinguish between four fundamental
   - ❑ a. smells.
   - ❑ b. emotions.
   - ❑ c. tastes.

4. Tiny hairlike structures attached to olfactory cells are called
   - ❑ a. filaments.
   - ❑ b. cilia.
   - ❑ c. taste buds.

5. Emotions are associated with a part of the brain called the
   - ❑ a. lymphatic system.
   - ❑ b. olfactory system.
   - ❑ c. limbic system.

Understanding Ideas

6. Which of the following statements is most likely true?
   - ❑ a. Men and women prefer completely different aromas.
   - ❑ b. Other species also have four basic tastes.
   - ❑ c. Flavors are created in part by the sense of smell.

7. The article suggests that if someone has a pleasant experience while sniffing a particular aroma, she or he
   - ❑ a. is likely to experience positive feelings when encountering the aroma again.
   - ❑ b. will not associate the aroma with the experience.
   - ❑ c. will remember the experience but not the aroma.

8. One can infer from the article that a person who has the flu most likely has a diminished sense of
   - ❑ a. smell only.
   - ❑ b. smell and taste.
   - ❑ c. taste only.

9. One can infer from the article that
   - ❑ a. most positive memories are related to particular aromas.
   - ❑ b. certain scents might bring back negative memories as well as positive ones.
   - ❑ c. some brands of perfume are popular with all men.

10. Strong smells are most likely caused
    - ❑ a. by high concentrations of certain molecules in the air.
    - ❑ b. by special types of cilia that are sensitive to certain smells.
    - ❑ c. by random interpretations by the brain.

Balance and Dizziness

Feelings of balance and dizziness originate in the inner ear in a structure known as the vestibular organ. The vestibular organ consists of a network of chambers within the bony areas of the inner ear on each side of the head. One part of the network consists of three semicircular canals that are at right angles to one another. These canals help the brain sense rotational movement. The other part of the network consists of two saclike structures that help sense linear movement. The entire network contains a thick fluid called endolymph. Cilia extend out from the walls of the network.

The way the brain detects a change in the body's position involves shifts in the endolymph. Whenever the body moves, the endolymph moves just a bit more slowly. The movement of the endolymph causes the cilia to move as well. This results in the cilia stimulating the cells to which they are attached. These cells engender nerve impulses that are transmitted to the brain. The brain interprets these impulses to determine the body's new position and make any necessary adjustments.

If the position of the body continuously changes, the reaction of the endolymph continuously lags behind. This creates an inconsistency between where the eyes are directed and where the brain expects the eyes to be directed. The inconsistency creates a feeling of dizziness. A common example is when a person turns in circles while standing in the same spot.

1. **Recognizing Words in Context**

   Find the word *engender* in the passage. One definition below is closest to the meaning of that word. One definition has the opposite or nearly opposite meaning. The remaining definition has a completely different meaning. Label the definitions C for *closest*, O for *opposite or nearly opposite*, and D for *different*.

   _____ a. eliminate

   _____ b. change

   _____ c. generate

2. **Distinguishing Fact from Opinion**

   Two of the statements below present *facts*, which can be proved *correct*. The other statement is an opinion, which expresses someone's thoughts or beliefs. Label the statements F for *fact* and O for *opinion*.

   _____ a. The fluid in the inner ear is called endolymph.

   _____ b. Cilia line the walls of the vestibular organ.

   _____ c. Few things are more unpleasant than dizziness.

3. Keeping Events in Order

Label the statements below 1, 2, and 3 to show the order in which the events happen.

_____ a. Cells in the inner ear send nerve impulses to the brain.

_____ b. The body changes position.

_____ c. Movements of the endolymph cause cilia to move.

4. Making Correct Inferences

Two of the statements below are correct *inferences,* or reasonable guesses. They are based on information in the passage. The other statement is an incorrect, or faulty, inference. Label the statements C for *correct* inference and F for *faulty* inference.

_____ a. Gravity determines the movement of the endolymph.

_____ b. The vestibular organ is also directly involved in hearing.

_____ c. Diseases of the inner ear can make it difficult for people to keep their balance.

5. Understanding Main Ideas

One of the statements below expresses the main idea of the passage. One statement is too general, or too broad. The other explains only part of the passage; it is too narrow. Label the statements M for *main idea*, B for *too broad*, and N for *too narrow*.

_____ a. The vestibular organ consists of a network of chambers.

_____ b. The inner ear is responsible for a person's sense of balance.

_____ c. The body's sense of balance depends on a fluid within the inner ear.

Correct Answers, Part A _____

Correct Answers, Part B _____

Total Correct Answers _____

22   A   Single-Celled Organisms

Biologists classify living organisms in a variety of ways. The science of biological classification is called taxonomy. Taxonomy is a controversial field because it is difficult to group living things into separate categories; many organisms are similar in some ways but different in others. One of the most common classification systems involves sorting organisms into five kingdoms based on the type and complexity of their cellular structures. Single-celled organisms comprise two of these kingdoms: Monera and Protista.

Most scientists classify cells as either prokaryotic or eukaryotic. Prokaryotic cells are simpler in structure. Although they have the genetic material called DNA, they lack the central nucleus found in eukaryotic cells. The DNA of prokaryotes floats freely around the cell.

The kingdom Monera is made up of bacteria, which are prokaryotic cells. The number of bacteria is far greater than the number of eukaryotic creatures. Monerans include bacteria that undergo photosynthesis, bacteria that decompose dead organisms, and bacteria that cause disease.

Monerans are among the most ancient of life forms, having been present on Earth for billions of years. They can reproduce by simple cell division every 20 minutes. They have high mutation rates, which means that they can quickly adapt to changes in their environment. Bacteria have even been able to adapt to such difficult environments as hot sulfur springs. Mutation also allows bacteria to become resistant to antibiotics, drugs that are created to destroy bacteria or prevent them from reproducing.

Pathogenic bacteria, the bacteria that cause disease, are found almost everywhere. Human immune systems are able to fight off most pathogenic bacteria. But if the body becomes stressed—for instance, through fatigue or improper nutrition—bacteria can reproduce rapidly and cause serious infections. Streptococcal bacteria make up one category of pathogenic bacteria. These bacteria, which have a chainlike appearance, typically live in the throats of healthy people. They can cause an ailment known as strep throat if the immune system becomes weakened.

The kingdom Protista also is made up of single-celled creatures. These organisms, however, are eukaryotic in nature: they have a central nucleus, organlike structures called organelles, and cells that are much larger than prokaryotic cells. This kingdom includes many pathogenic organisms as well, such as those that cause malaria, a serious blood disease, and giardiasis, a disease of the intestines. Some other protists have plantlike characteristics and make up part of the plankton, a food source for marine animals.

Reading Time _____

Recalling Facts

1. Biologists classify living organisms into groups known as
   - ❑ a. herds.
   - ❑ b. organelles.
   - ❑ c. kingdoms.

2. Cells that lack a nucleus are known as
   - ❑ a. eukaryotes.
   - ❑ b. prokaryotes.
   - ❑ c. fungi.

3. The term *pathogenic* means
   - ❑ a. disease causing.
   - ❑ b. decomposing.
   - ❑ c. bacterial.

4. Single-celled organisms make up _____ of the five kingdoms of living things.
   - ❑ a. one
   - ❑ b. two
   - ❑ c. three

5. Bacteria can adapt quickly to changes in their environment because they
   - ❑ a. have high mutation rates.
   - ❑ b. have highly evolved brainlike structures.
   - ❑ c. choose to live in environments that change very slowly.

Understanding Ideas

6. From the information in the article, one can conclude that when bacteria mutate,
   - ❑ a. they are no longer bacteria.
   - ❑ b. their characteristics change.
   - ❑ c. they usually lose any pathogenic qualities they may have.

7. One can infer that biologists
   - ❑ a. have reached a consensus about the correct number of kingdoms of living things.
   - ❑ b. disagree about how to divide living things into kingdoms.
   - ❑ c. have not yet decided whether *kingdoms* is a proper term to use.

8. The DNA in a eukaryotic cell is found in the
   - ❑ a. organelle.
   - ❑ b. cell wall.
   - ❑ c. nucleus.

9. One can conclude that single-celled organisms
   - ❑ a. are nearly identical.
   - ❑ b. can vary widely in characteristics.
   - ❑ c. are all potentially dangerous.

10. A person would be most likely to get a bacterial infection if he or she
    - ❑ a. went swimming in water that was full of plankton.
    - ❑ b. is related to someone who had a bacterial infection in the previous year.
    - ❑ c. refused to eat any fruits or vegetables.

Types of Monerans

Monerans are some of the most diverse and successful species on the planet. They constitute the most ancient form of life on Earth. Monerans are defined as single-celled prokaryotic organisms. Also called prokaryotes, these organisms have a simple cellular structure. Many biologists classify monerans into two distinct groups, eubacteria and archaebacteria. These two groups differ in cellular chemistries and processes. For example, the cell walls of eubacteria and archaebacteria are made up of different materials.

Eubacteria consist of some 5,000 species, each of which are cells with circular strands of DNA and a cell wall that serves as the boundary of each cell. Eubacteria can have spherical, rodlike, or spiral shapes, and they usually reproduce by simple cell division. Some eubacteria are especially important and beneficial for their role in decomposing, or breaking down, dead plants and animals. Other eubacteria cause dangerous diseases.

Archaebacteria, or archaea as they are sometimes called, were the earliest monerans. These organisms are found in onerous environments where few other creatures can live. This group includes the methanogens, which aid digestion in the intestines of animals while creating methane gas. Also belonging to this group are the halophiles, or "salt-loving" creatures, which live in salt water, and the thermophiles, or "heat-loving" creatures, which live in hot sulfur springs.

1. **Recognizing Words in Context**

   Find the word *onerous* in the passage. One definition below is closest to the meaning of that word. One definition has the opposite or nearly opposite meaning. The remaining definition has a completely different meaning. Label the definitions C for *closest*, O for *opposite or nearly opposite*, and D for *different*.

   _____ a. hospitable

   _____ b. hot

   _____ c. difficult

2. **Distinguishing Fact from Opinion**

   Two of the statements below present *facts*, which can be proved correct. The other statement is an *opinion*, which expresses someone's thoughts or beliefs. Label the statements F for *fact* and O for *opinion*.

   _____ a. Monerans that decompose dead organisms are the most important living things on Earth.

   _____ b. Some eubacteria cause disease.

   _____ c. Monerans are prokaryotic.

3. Keeping Events in Order

Label the statements below 1, 2, and 3 to show the order in which the events happen.

_____ a. A plant dies.

_____ b. Bacteria break the plant down into organic substances.

_____ c. Soil is fertilized by organic substances.

4. Making Correct Inferences

Two of the statements below are correct *inferences*, or reasonable guesses. They are based on information in the passage. The other statement is an incorrect, or faulty, inference. Label the statements C for *correct* inference and F for *faulty* inference.

_____ a. Some bacteria are beneficial and some are harmful.

_____ b. No organisms other than archaebacteria live in the intestines of animals.

_____ c. Monerans are among the simplest of all living things.

5. Understanding Main Ideas

One of the statements below expresses the main idea of the passage. One statement is too general, or too broad. The other explains only part of the passage; it is too narrow. Label the statements M for *main idea*, B for *too broad*, and N for *too narrow*.

_____ a. Monerans form the kingdom that is made up of the many types of bacteria.

_____ b. Methanogens live in the intestines of some animals.

_____ c. Some organisms are made up of a single cell.

Correct Answers, Part A _____

Correct Answers, Part B _____

Total Correct Answers _____

Wireless communication is a type of technology that allows people to communicate without using cables or telephone lines. In the past, people had to be in a building or at a phone booth to send or receive information. The development of cellular telephones changed all that and ushered in a revolution that has had a dramatic impact on millions of people's lives, especially in the world of business. Nearly anywhere they go, people with cell phones can be reached with important information or questions.

Wireless technology uses electromagnetic radiation to transmit information. In this way it is nearly identical to radio broadcasting. Radio waves are used to transmit information to both radios and cell phones. The difference is that cell phones can send radio waves as well as receive them.

The development of satellite communications made the success of cell phones possible. Radio waves cannot travel along a curved path, and so, in the past, radio communication was limited by the curvature of Earth. Radio broadcasts could not be transmitted from the United States to China, for example. But with satellites, radio waves can be transmitted toward outer space and then be sent back down to the other side of the planet. In most populated areas, companies have constructed antennae for transmitting cellular phone signals back and forth from satellites. Despite the advances, however, the technology is still limited. Tall buildings and bad weather can easily disrupt a signal, and range is often restricted.

Also, because of current restraints, only a small amount of data per second can be sent with wireless devices. Even so, handheld computers and personal assistant devices, designed to allow people to access their e-mail and the Internet without cable connections, have become quite popular.

One day, using handheld wireless devices may become the most common way for people to shop, make reservations, or access weather and news information. For now, some sectors of the wireless industry have been held back by high costs and slow speed.

In the United States, slow speed has been a big problem with handheld Web browsers. In regions like Japan and Scandinavia, these devices are much more popular and efficient then they are here. One reason is that these places have created technological specifications that make all wireless devices compatible with one another. In contrast, the United States allows companies to use a variety of specifications, and the incompatibility of devices is a major issue.

Reading Time _____

Recalling Facts

1. The success of _____ marked the beginning of the wireless communication revolution.
   - ❑ a. personal computers
   - ❑ b. cell phones
   - ❑ c. handheld wireless devices

2. To transmit signals, wireless systems use
   - ❑ a. radio waves.
   - ❑ b. electronic pulses.
   - ❑ c. cable modems.

3. According to the article, handheld wireless devices are especially popular in
   - ❑ a. Russia.
   - ❑ b. France.
   - ❑ c. Japan.

4. A major obstacle within the wireless industry is
   - ❑ a. a shortage of satellites.
   - ❑ b. the incompatibility of devices.
   - ❑ c. the availability of cell phones.

5. The article states that cellular phone signals can be disrupted by
   - ❑ a. tall buildings.
   - ❑ b. satellite incompatibility.
   - ❑ c. radio broadcasts.

Understanding Ideas

6. It can be inferred that
   - ❑ a. wireless communication is used in every region of the world.
   - ❑ b. countries vary widely in their use of wireless communication.
   - ❑ c. wireless technology is likely to lose popularity in the future.

7. The most likely result of the standardization of U.S. wireless technology would be an increase in
   - ❑ a. concern about technology taking over society.
   - ❑ b. the costs of wireless technology for the next 100 years.
   - ❑ c. the usage of handheld wireless devices.

8. The article suggests that
   - ❑ a. handheld wireless devices may improve people's lives.
   - ❑ b. it will be a long time before efficient handheld wireless devices are developed.
   - ❑ c. cellular phones get better reception in rural areas.

9. Which is most likely true?
   - ❑ a. Wireless technology is too expensive for almost everyone.
   - ❑ b. There is great demand for existing wireless technology.
   - ❑ c. Some people are not interested in wireless technology.

10. One can assume that
   - ❑ a. the transmission of data is faster now than in the past.
   - ❑ b. people prefer to receive news stories through wireless devices.
   - ❑ c. people in Scandinavia are smarter than other people.

23 | B | The Future of Wireless Communication

The field of wireless communication seems to offer limitless opportunities. As the technology improves, not only will people be able to perform a number of routine tasks by using a handheld wireless device, but they will also be able to perform tasks that have not yet even been thought of.

The problem of slow speed is one of the major drawbacks in wireless communication, but it is gradually being addressed and resolved. Another problem is that wireless devices can use radio waves with only a small range of wavelengths, which limits the technology. A technology called 3G, or third-generation, wireless systems has recently been deployed in Japan. This innovative system is expected to spread through both Europe and the United States within the next few years.

The new 3G technology is designed to carry both digital data and voice messages. It will increase download speed to 2.4 megabits per second, twice as fast as current cable-modem speeds. It will also be upgradable, allow people to use more than one Web browser, and give them the ability to download games, music, and video—all through a simple handheld device. This technology, and others still to come, will one day cause people to wonder how they ever got along without wireless communications.

1. **Recognizing Words in Context**

    Find the word *deployed* in the passage. One definition below is closest to the meaning of that word. One definition has the opposite or nearly opposite meaning. The remaining definition has a completely different meaning. Label the definitions C for *closest*, O for *opposite or nearly opposite*, and D for *different*.

    _____ a. put in place

    _____ b. removed

    _____ c. linked

2. **Distinguishing Fact from Opinion**

    Two of the statements below present *facts*, which can be proved correct. The other statement is an *opinion*, which expresses someone's thoughts or beliefs. Label the statements F for *fact* and O for *opinion*.

    _____ a. New technologies are constantly evolving.

    _____ b. 3G technology is the best wireless communication standard ever developed.

    _____ c. Slow speed has been an obstacle for users of handheld wireless devices.

3. Keeping Events in Order

Label the statements below 1, 2, and 3 to show the order in which the events happen.

_____ a. 3G wireless systems become widely used in the wireless industry.

_____ b. Cellular phones are developed.

_____ c. Radio waves are first used for broadcasting.

4. Making Correct Inferences

Two of the statements below are correct *inferences,* or reasonable guesses. They are based on information in the passage. The other statement is an incorrect, or faulty, inference. Label the statements C for *correct* inference and F for *faulty* inference.

_____ a. Wireless communication will be more effective in the future than it is today.

_____ b. 3G technology will eliminate wireless communication problems.

_____ c. Increasing the speed of wireless devices will make them more useful to people.

5. Understanding Main Ideas

One of the statements below expresses the main idea of the passage. One statement is too general, or too broad. The other explains only part of the passage; it is too narrow. Label the statements M for *main idea,* B for *too broad,* and N for *too narrow.*

_____ a. Communication technology has evolved rapidly.

_____ b. 3G technology has been deployed in Japan.

_____ c. The future of wireless communication appears promising.

Correct Answers, Part A _____

Correct Answers, Part B _____

Total Correct Answers _____

Plants undergo a predictable cycle of changes with the passage of seasons. Changes can be especially dramatic in the periods leading up to and following winter, when many plants undergo a period of dormancy. The degree of change varies not only with the type of plant but also with the degree of regional difference between summer and winter conditions.

Deciduous trees—trees that shed their leaves in autumn—display a series of colors as they adapt to temperature variations. These colors result from biochemical changes within the tree. During photosynthesis, a deciduous tree absorbs energy from the sun into the green pigment of its leaves and uses this energy to power chemical reactions that create its food. The green pigment is called chlorophyll. Each tree leaf has millions of chloroplasts, tiny structures that contain chlorophyll. The needles of pine trees and other conifers also contain chlorophyll.

As temperatures decrease toward the end of summer, the colors of the leaves of deciduous trees begin to change. In spring and summer, these leaves contain pigments of orange, red, and yellow as well as green, but the green pigment masks the other colors because there is far more of it. Chlorophyll production is driven by temperature, and so as the temperature falls the amount of chlorophyll in leaves decreases. As the green pigment of the leaves dissipates, the vibrant pigments of orange, red, and yellow become increasingly prominent.

It would do no good for deciduous trees to maintain their leaves through the winter, because winter frost can kill leaves. The trees adapt to the loss of food-production capability during the winter by slowing their metabolisms, just as most animals slow their metabolisms during winter. The tree is able to store some of the food it produces during spring and summer for use in winter. Special tissue in the trunk and branches store the food.

Like deciduous trees, other plants undergo seasonal alterations. Many plants react to temperature increases in the midsummer and have developed mechanisms to protect themselves from the severe heat of the sun. For example, desert cacti open their stomata at night but close them during the day. Stomata are small pores that allow a plant to exchange gases with the outside environment. This gas exchange is necessary for the vital processes of the plant's cells. By closing their stomata during the day, cacti minimize the loss of water through evaporation.

Reading Time _____

Recalling Facts

1. During photosynthesis, plants use the sun's energy to create
   - ❏ a. pigment.
   - ❏ b. food.
   - ❏ c. roots.

2. Plant leaves that are green get their color from a pigment known as
   - ❏ a. chlorophyll.
   - ❏ b. carotene.
   - ❏ c. stomata.

3. Pigments in leaves include all of the following colors except
   - ❏ a. yellow.
   - ❏ b. blue.
   - ❏ c. red.

4. Plants exchange gases with the atmosphere through their
   - ❏ a. bark.
   - ❏ b. food-storage tissue.
   - ❏ c. stomata.

5. Many living things _____ their metabolisms during winter.
   - ❏ a. speed up
   - ❏ b. eliminate
   - ❏ c. slow down

Understanding Ideas

6. One can infer that the colors of autumn leaves are strongest in areas that have
   - ❏ a. warm autumns.
   - ❏ b. cool autumns.
   - ❏ c. hot autumns.

7. It can be inferred that if leaves on a tree appear orange, red, and yellow,
   - ❏ a. they are full of chlorophyll.
   - ❏ b. those types of leaves never had chlorophyll to begin with.
   - ❏ c. they have less chlorophyll in their leaves than other pigments.

8. According to the article,
   - ❏ a. the metabolic needs of plants vary with environmental conditions.
   - ❏ b. each kind of pigment within a leaf can convert the sun's energy into food.
   - ❏ c. the level of chlorophyll in leaves is highest in autumn.

9. One can infer from the article that pine needles produce less food in winter because
   - ❏ a. the needles fall off the tree.
   - ❏ b. there are fewer hours of daylight in the winter.
   - ❏ c. most pine needles do not contain chlorophyll.

10. The article suggests that desert plants
    - ❏ a. have lower energy requirements than other plants.
    - ❏ b. have been able to adapt to harsh environments.
    - ❏ c. do not undergo photosynthesis.

24 B The Mayapple

Deep within the deciduous forests of North America, especially in the midwestern United States, large patches of mayapple can be found. These small plants grow in the moist undergrowth of huge trees, and, depending on the season, they can look like mundane green plants or exhibit flowers or fruit.

It is during the early spring that the mayapple comes to life; it begins by growing a shoot that resembles a closed umbrella. After the shoot reaches a height of approximately 30 centimeters (12 inches), the shoot slowly unfolds. At the junction between two shoots, a six-petaled white flower emerges. The flower quickly dies, and in its place a lemon-shaped fruit develops. The fruit is green, and its flesh is similar to that of an apple. The fruit continues to mature until it reaches the size of a large strawberry. At this time the fruit falls off, and the life cycle begins again.

The fruit that mayapples produce are edible, and some people make them into jam. The rest of the plant is poisonous, including the leaves, stems, and roots. The rhizome is thought to have medicinal value. The rhizome is the underground stem from which the roots develop. Compounds created from the ground rhizome are used in the treatment of bacterial infections and tumors.

1. **Recognizing Words in Context**

   Find the word *mundane* in the passage. One definition below is closest to the meaning of that word. One definition has the opposite or nearly opposite meaning. The remaining definition has a completely different meaning. Label the definitions C for *closest*, O for *opposite or nearly opposite*, and D for *different*.

   _____ a. extraordinary

   _____ b. fertile

   _____ c. unremarkable

2. **Distinguishing Fact from Opinion**

   Two of the statements below present *facts*, which can be proved correct. The other statement is an *opinion*, which expresses someone's thoughts or beliefs. Label the statements F for *fact* and O for *opinion*.

   _____ a. The mayapple is an outstanding example of a seasonal plant.

   _____ b. The mayapple produces a fruit that can be used in jam.

   _____ c. The mayapple produces a six-petaled white flower.

3. Keeping Events in Order

Label the statements below 1, 2, and 3 to show the order in which the events happen.

_____ a. A six-petaled flower emerges.

_____ b. A mayapple shoot forms.

_____ c. A mayapple fruit grows to a size of a large strawberry.

4. Making Correct Inferences

Two of the statements below are correct *inferences*, or reasonable guesses. They are based on information in the passage. The other statement is an incorrect, or faulty, inference. Label the statements C for *correct* inference and F for *faulty* inference.

_____ a. The mayapple's appearance changes during the year.

_____ b. Medicines made from the mayapple can be found in several sections of any drugstore.

_____ c. People do not make jam out of the mayapple's leaves, stems, or roots.

5. Understanding Main Ideas

One of the statements below expresses the main idea of the passage. One statement is too general, or too broad. The other explains only part of the passage; it is too narrow. Label the statements M for *main idea*, B for *too broad*, and N for *too narrow*.

_____ a. The mayapple is an example of a seasonal woodland plant.

_____ b. There are some plants that vary with the seasons.

_____ c. The mayapple sometimes has a six-petaled white flower.

Correct Answers, Part A _____

Correct Answers, Part B _____

Total Correct Answers _____

A volcano is the result of a cauldron of activity deep beneath Earth's surface. Molten rock called magma churns and rises, causing colder and heavier crust to fall in its place. This process whereby warmer, lighter rock rises as cooler, heavier rock falls is called convection. This convection brings about heat transfer and is responsible for many of Earth's dynamic processes, such as the occurrences of earthquakes and the eruptions of volcanoes.

Earth is composed of rocky material that exists as either a solid or liquid depending on its temperature, pressure, and chemical composition. Earth's outer layer, called the crust or lithosphere, is rocky in consistency and floats above a semifluid layer called the asthenosphere. The asthenosphere is partly fluid because of the tremendous temperature and pressure deep within Earth's core. Large temperature differences also exist within the asthenosphere, causing the molten fluid inside it to flow.

Usually heat flow within an object does not cause significant exterior changes. This is not the case with Earth's heat flow, however. Because of cracks that extend through Earth's crust, the flow of magma is not contained within the asthenosphere but rises to Earth's surface. The liquid magma melts additional rock during its journey to the surface, and when it finally reaches the surface as lava, it is released under pressure—sometimes tremendous pressure. The area in the surface where the magma is released is called a volcano.

There are several types of volcanoes. A shield volcano results from layers of low-viscosity, or highly fluid, magma that has reached the surface of Earth and hardened with each successive flow. Shield volcanoes are seldom dangerous because the gas within the thin magma can escape easily at the beginning of an eruption. These volcanoes tend to be broad with low slopes.

More violent eruptions occur with stratovolcanoes. Stratovolcanoes contain a magma that is very viscous with a consistency similar to that of molasses. This type of magma produces more powerful eruptions because the high-viscosity magma does not allow gas to escape readily. Instead, the pressure builds until it reaches a level strong enough to burst through the rock in an explosion of gas, magma, rock fragments, and ash.

The smallest and most common type of volcano is the scoria cone. This type of volcano has steep slopes and consists of piles of basalt rock. It results from semiviscous magma that produces small explosions.

Reading Time _____

Recalling Facts

1. Earth's outer layer is called the
   - ❑ a. subsoil.
   - ❑ b. crust.
   - ❑ c. asthenosphere.

2. Heat transfer within Earth occurs by a process known as
   - ❑ a. conduction.
   - ❑ b. convection.
   - ❑ c. radiation.

3. The asthenosphere is _____ in nature.
   - ❑ a. solid
   - ❑ b. semifluid
   - ❑ c. gaseous

4. Low-viscosity magma is typically released from
   - ❑ a. large explosions of rock.
   - ❑ b. stratovolcanoes.
   - ❑ c. shield volcanoes.

5. Molten rock within Earth is also called
   - ❑ a. crust.
   - ❑ b. magma.
   - ❑ c. basalt.

Understanding Ideas

6. That the interior of Earth is constantly changing implies that
   - ❑ a. thunderstorms transfer some of their energy below ground.
   - ❑ b. Earth is full of pressure and temperature variances.
   - ❑ c. heat tranfer in the atmosphere causes instability.

7. The most likely result of an upward flow of highly viscous magma is
   - ❑ a. an increase in pressure on the surface.
   - ❑ b. a volcanic eruption that kills thousands of people.
   - ❑ c. the creation of deep canyons at the surface.

8. The article suggests that if there were no cracks in Earth's crust,
   - ❑ a. most volcanoes would be shield volcanoes.
   - ❑ b. volcanoes would not exist.
   - ❑ c. there would be only two or three gigantic volcanoes.

9. If you found out that heat can make motor oil thinner, you would want to
   - ❑ a. use a more viscous motor oil during the summer.
   - ❑ b. use a less viscous motor oil during the summer.
   - ❑ c. add water to motor oil.

10. The article suggests that
    - ❑ a. many temperature zones exist within Earth.
    - ❑ b. the area beneath the lithosphere is pure magma.
    - ❑ c. the Earth will become less active over time.

In western Indonesia, between the large islands of Java and Sumatra, sits a volcanic island called Krakatoa. The island is only 13 square kilometers (5 square miles) in area and rises to a height of only 810 meters (2,667 feet). But it was once much larger. A huge volcanic explosion in 1883 destroyed not only most of Krakatoa but also much of the adjacent strait.

The eruption of the Krakatoa volcano was probably the most powerful volcanic explosion of modern times. The blast released huge amounts of rock, ash, lava, and gas, and it caused widespread ruin. The blast created a huge wave, or tsunami, that reached a height of 34 meters (112 feet), as tall as a building 11 stories high. The tsunami caused massive flooding on nearby islands and destroyed many coastal communities. The volcano's eruption was so large that an area of about 780 square kilometers (300 square miles) around it was covered with volcanic ash, and the explosion was heard as far away as the Philippine Islands. The explosion was also said to have had a force greater than 21,000 times that of an atomic bomb. So much ash entered the atmosphere that it blocked out the sun in some areas and caused worldwide climate changes for months.

1. **Recognizing Words in Context**

   Find the word *adjacent* in the passage. One definition below is closest to the meaning of that word. One definition has the opposite or nearly opposite meaning. The remaining definition has a completely different meaning. Label the definitions C for *closest*, O for *opposite or nearly opposite*, and D for *different*.

   _____ a. distant

   _____ b. nearby

   _____ c. curving

2. **Distinguishing Fact from Opinion**

   Two of the statements below present *facts*, which can be proved correct. The other statement is an *opinion*, which expresses someone's thoughts or beliefs. Label the statements F for *fact* and O for *opinion*.

   _____ a. The island of Krakatoa is volcanic in origin.

   _____ b. The 1883 eruption of Krakatoa was the most devastating natural disaster of modern times.

   _____ c. A giant wave is sometimes called a tsunami.

3. Keeping Events in Order

Two of the statements below describe events that happened at the same time. The other statement describes an event that happened before or after those events. Label them S for *same time,* B for *before,* or A for *after.*

_____ a. Krakatoa began to erupt.

_____ b. A tsunami formed.

_____ c. Rock flew through the air.

4. Making Correct Inferences

Two of the statements below are correct *inferences,* or reasonable guesses. They are based on information in the passage. The other statement is an incorrect, or faulty, inference. Label the statements C for *correct* inference and F for *faulty* inference.

_____ a. Every volcanic eruption has an explosive force greater than an atomic bomb.

_____ b. Java and Sumatra were covered by volcanic ash after Krakatoa erupted.

_____ c. Tsunamis can cause flooding in coastal communities.

5. Understanding Main Ideas

One of the statements below expresses the main idea of the passage. One statement is too general, or too broad. The other explains only part of the passage; it is too narrow. Label the statements M for *main idea,* B for *too broad,* and N for *too narrow.*

_____ a. The 1883 eruption of Krakatoa was very powerful and caused widespread devastation.

_____ b. The island of Krakatoa is volcanic.

_____ c. The eruption of Krakatoa affected the weather.

Correct Answers, Part A _____

Correct Answers, Part B _____

Total Correct Answers _____

ANSWER KEY

READING RATE GRAPH

COMPREHENSION SCORE GRAPH

COMPREHENSION SKILLS PROFILE GRAPH

ANSWER KEY

1A	1. a	2. c	3. b	4. a	5. c	6. b	7. b	8. b	9. a	10. a
1B	1. C, D, O	2. F, O, F	3. 1, 3, 2	4. C, F, C	5. B, M, N
2A	1. a	2. b	3. c	4. b	5. b	6. b	7. c	8. b	9. b	10. a
2B	1. C, O, D	2. O, F, F	3. 2, 3, 1	4. C, C, F	5. M, B, N
3A	1. c	2. b	3. a	4. b	5. a	6. b	7. b	8. a	9. c	10. b
3B	1. O, D, C	2. O, F, F	3. 2, 3, 1	4. C, F, C	5. M, B, N
4A	1. b	2. c	3. b	4. a	5. c	6. a	7. b	8. c	9. a	10. c
4B	1. O, C, D	2. O, F, F	3. 2, 1, 3	4. C, C, F	5. N, M, B
5A	1. a	2. b	3. b	4. c	5. b	6. a	7. b	8. b	9. b	10. a
5B	1. O, D, C	2. F, F, O	3. 1, 3, 2	4. F, C, C	5. B, M, N
6A	1. b	2. a	3. c	4. a	5. a	6. b	7. b	8. c	9. c	10. b
6B	1. O, C, D	2. O, F, F	3. 2, 3, 1	4. F, C, C	5. N, B, M
7A	1. b	2. a	3. b	4. c	5. c	6. b	7. c	8. a	9. b	10. b
7B	1. C, D, O	2. F, F, O	3. 1, 3, 2	4. C, F, C	5. B, N, M
8A	1. b	2. b	3. b	4. c	5. a	6. b	7. b	8. a	9. b	10. c
8B	1. O, D, C	2. F, F, O	3. 1, 2, 3	4. C, F, C	5. B, N, M
9A	1. a	2. b	3. b	4. b	5. c	6. c	7. a	8. b	9. a	10. a
9B	1. O, C, D	2. F, F, O	3. S, A, S	4. F, C, C	5. N, M, B
10A	1. b	2. a	3. b	4. a	5. c	6. a	7. a	8. b	9. c	10. b
10B	1. D, C, O	2. F, O, F	3. 3, 1, 2	4. C, F, C	5. B, M, N
11A	1. a	2. b	3. b	4. b	5. c	6. c	7. b	8. a	9. b	10. a
11B	1. D, O, C	2. O, F, F	3. 2, 3, 1	4. C, F, C	5. M, N, B
12A	1. c	2. a	3. b	4. a	5. c	6. b	7. a	8. b	9. b	10. c
12B	1. C, O, D	2. O, F, F	3. 3, 1, 2	4. C, F, C	5. B, M, N
13A	1. a	2. b	3. a	4. c	5. a	6. c	7. b	8. b	9. a	10. c
13B	1. O, D, C	2. F, O, F	3. 1, 3, 2	4. F, C, C	5. B, M, N

14A	1. b	2. a	3. b	4. a	5. c	6. a	7. c	8. b	9. a	10. a
14B	1. C, D, O	2. F, F, O	3. 2, 1, 3	4. F, C, C	5. N, M, B					
15A	1. a	2. b	3. b	4. b	5. c	6. b	7. c	8. b	9. c	10. b
15B	1. D, O, C	2. F, O, F	3. 2, 1, 3	4. C, C, F	5. B, N, M					
16A	1. b	2. a	3. b	4. a	5. c	6. c	7. a	8. b	9. c	10. b
16B	1. D, O, C	2. F, O, F	3. 2, 1, 3	4. C, F, C	5. B, M, N					
17A	1. a	2. a	3. b	4. c	5. c	6. b	7. a	8. c	9. b	10. c
17B	1. C, O, D	2. F, F, O	3. 1, 3, 2	4. C, F, C	5. M, B, N					
18A	1. b	2. a	3. c	4. c	5. b	6. b	7. c	8. c	9. c	10. a
18B	1. O, C, D	2. O, F, F	3. 2, 3, 1	4. F, C, C	5. M, B, N					
19A	1. c	2. b	3. c	4. b	5. a	6. b	7. a	8. c	9. b	10. b
19B	1. C, D, O	2. O, F, F	3. 3, 2, 1	4. C, F, C	5. B, N, M					
20A	1. b	2. c	3. c	4. b	5. c	6. a	7. b	8. b	9. b	10. a
20B	1. C, D, O	2. F, O, F	3. 1, 2, 3	4. C, F, C	5. B, N, M					
21A	1. a	2. b	3. c	4. b	5. c	6. c	7. a	8. b	9. b	10. a
21B	1. O, D, C	2. F, F, O	3. 3, 1, 2	4. C, C, F	5. N, B, M					
22A	1. c	2. b	3. a	4. b	5. a	6. b	7. b	8. c	9. b	10. c
22B	1. O, D, C	2. O, F, F	3. 1, 2, 3	4. C, F, C	5. M, N, B					
23A	1. b	2. a	3. c	4. b	5. a	6. b	7. c	8. a	9. c	10. a
23B	1. C, O, D	2. F, O, F	3. 3, 2, 1	4. C, F, C	5. B, N, M					
24A	1. b	2. a	3. b	4. c	5. c	6. b	7. c	8. a	9. b	10. b
24B	1. O, D, C	2. O, F, F	3. 2, 1, 3	4. C, F, C	5. M, B, N					
25A	1. b	2. b	3. b	4. c	5. b	6. b	7. a	8. b	9. a	10. b
25B	1. O, C, D	2. F, O, F	3. B, S, S	4. F, C, C	5. M, B, N					

READING RATE

Put an X on the line above each lesson number to show your reading time and words-per-minute rate for that lesson.

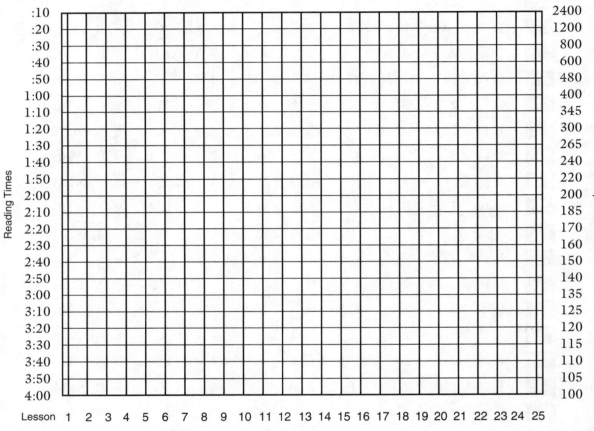

Reading Times		Words per Minute
:10		2400
:20		1200
:30		800
:40		600
:50		480
1:00		400
1:10		345
1:20		300
1:30		265
1:40		240
1:50		220
2:00		200
2:10		185
2:20		170
2:30		160
2:40		150
2:50		140
3:00		135
3:10		125
3:20		120
3:30		115
3:40		110
3:50		105
4:00		100

Lesson 1 2 3 4 5 6 7 8 9 10 11 12 13 14 15 16 17 18 19 20 21 22 23 24 25

COMPREHENSION SCORE

Put an X on the line above each lesson number to indicate your total correct answers and comprehension score for that lesson.

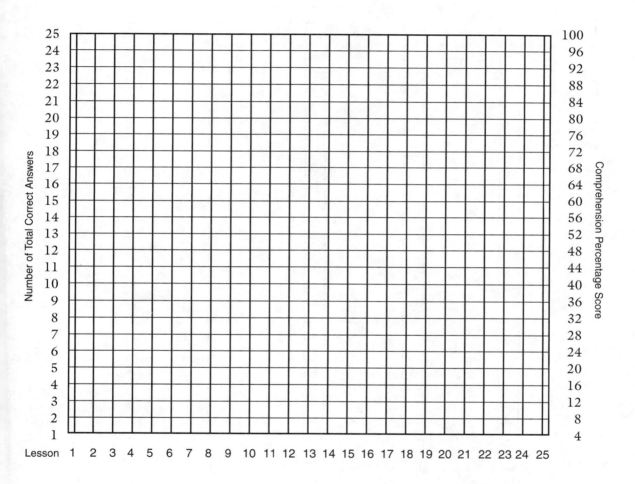

COMPREHENSION SKILLS PROFILE

Put an X in the box above each question type to indicate an incorrect reponse to any part of that question.

Lesson 1					
2					
3					
4					
5					
6					
7					
8					
9					
10					
11					
12					
13					
14					
15					
16					
17					
18					
19					
20					
21					
22					
23					
24					
25					
	Recognizing Words in Context	Distinguishing Fact from Opinion	Keeping Events in Order	Making Correct Inferences	Understanding Main Ideas